FREEDOM FEMINISM
Its Surprising History and Why It Matters Today

FREEDOM FEMINISM
Its Surprising History and Why It Matters Today

Christina Hoff Sommers

AEI Press
Washington, D.C.

Distributed by arrangement with the Rowan & Littlefield Publishing Group, 4501 Forbes Boulevard, Suite 200, Lanham, MD 20706. To order call toll free 1-800-462-6420 or 1-717-794-3800.

For all other inquiries please contact AEI Press, 1150 17th Street, N.W., Washington, D.C. 20036 or call 1-800-862-5801.

Sommers, Christina Hoff.
  Freedom feminism : its surprising history and why it matters today / by Christina Hoff Sommers.
     pages cm
  Includes bibliographical references.
  ISBN-13: 978-0-8447-7262-2 (pbk.)
  ISBN-10: 0-8447-7262-3 (pbk.)
  ISBN-13: 978-0-8447-7263-9 (ebook)
  ISBN-10: 0-8447-7263-1 (ebook) 1. Feminism--United States.
  2. Feminist theory--United States. 3. Feminism--
  United States--History.
  I. Title.
  HQ1421.S66 2013
  305.420973--dc23

CONTENTS

INTRODUCTION

If someone asked, "Are you a feminist?" how would you respond? Most Americans—including large majorities of women—say no. In recent surveys, 70 percent of women rejected the label (17 percent regarded it as an insult), while only 17 percent said they would welcome their daughter calling herself a feminist.[1] Accomplished modern women as diverse as Taylor Swift, Sandra Day O'Connor, Beyoncé, Sarah Jessica Parker, Carla Bruni-Sarkozy, Gwyneth Paltrow, Katy Perry, Yahoo CEO Marissa Mayer, and Lady Gaga object to the designation.[2] Why should that be so? The emancipation of women is one of the glories of Western civilization. Women organized, fought for, and won the right to vote and full equality before the law, the freedom to pursue an education and to enter any occupation, and the establishment of special protections against discrimination and harassment. Their deeds, some of them within living memory, profoundly improved society, government, and the economy. Feminism is one of the great chapters in the history of freedom. Why is the term that describes that heritage in such disrepute?

Terry O'Neill, president of the National Organization for Women (NOW), the largest feminist organization in the United States, claims that feminists have been unfairly portrayed as "unhappy, angry, humorless."[3] These stereotypes, she says, have estranged the younger generation. But are the stereotypes really unfounded? Consider the famous feminist playwright, Eve Ensler, lecturing at Harvard's Radcliffe Institute in 2003. She suggested that American women are just as oppressed as those in societies that practice acid burning and genital mutilation. "I think that the oppression of women is universal," Ensler said. "We are bonded in every single place of the world. I think conditions are *exactly* the same [her emphasis]. . . . The systematic global oppression of women is completely across the globe."[4]

The feminist blogger Jessica Valenti made a similar point in a 2010 *Washington Post* essay:

> We have no problem condemning atrocities done to women abroad, yet too many of us in the United States ignore the oppression on our doorstep. We're suffering under the mass delusion that women in America have achieved equality. . . . Part of this unwillingness to see misogyny in America could be self-protection—perhaps the truth is too scary to face.[5]

The African-American feminist bell hooks, Distinguished Professor of English at the City College of New York, has rightly criticized theories of "common oppression" for ignoring critical differences between the lives of poor women of color and those of privileged, college-educated, white women.[6] From hooks' perspective, sweeping pronouncements like Ensler's and Valenti's are elitist and out of touch. But hooks has contrived a radical theory of oppression even more alienating and removed from reality than those she criticizes. Says hooks, "As long as the United States is an imperialist, capitalist, patriarchal society, no large female majority can enter the existing ranks of the powerful."[7] She gratefully quotes French feminist Antoinette Fouque, who calls for the overthrow of the "phallic masculine economy."[8]

Fair or not, feminism is associated in the public mind with hardliners like Ensler, Valenti, and hooks. Most American women, including those strongly committed to equality, do not think of themselves as being in thrall to a mass delusion or held down by a system of global oppression. Asian, black, Latino, and white women want their basic rights, but hooks' call to bring down the "ruling capitalist patriarchy" is off-putting to most of them. To identify oneself as a feminist these days is to claim association with a dire worldview. So women of all colors tend to keep their distance. As for men, the vast majority have run for cover.

The major battles of American women for

equality and opportunity have been fought and won. Women in the United States have their freedom; they have achieved or exceeded parity with men in most ways. For combating the inequities that remain, it hardly helps to pretend that women's progress has all been illusory.

Some will ask, if the feminist movement has achieved its essential goals, why not let it fade from the scene? Thank you very much, now good-bye. That is an understandable but mistaken reaction. Feminism remains relevant and important in twenty-first century America for three reasons.

First, women in Western countries did form a movement and liberate themselves. That story has been vital to the evolution of liberal society. We should honor them, of course—but, even more, we should learn from them. Freedom in all of its forms requires continuing vigilance. The equal citizenship and social status that Western women have won should not be taken for granted. We need to understand how the women's movement succeeded in order to preserve and build on its achievements.

Second, for most of the world's women, the quest for equality has hardly begun. Across the globe, there are fledgling women's rights groups struggling to survive in the face of imprisonment and great suffering. Many of their leaders need and want our assistance.[9] Western women have a responsibility to help and much to offer. As it happens, the success of Western feminism provides a tried-and-true road map for women's movements in the developing world.

Third, even in the West, feminism's work is never done. Women, far more than men, struggle with the challenge of combining work and family. Our popular culture contains strong elements of misogyny. Although violence against women appears to be diminishing, it continues to exact a terrible toll. These problems are intractable and abiding. The negotiation of social and sexual relations between males and females is a constant feature of human existence. The unique circumstances of women require special attention and protections.

Who needs feminism? We do. The world does. But an effective women's movement needs to be rescued from its current outcast state. Feminism needs to become expansive and hospitable to the great majority of women whose sensibilities are moderate and customary rather than radical. That, indeed, is the great lesson of the historic women's movement. It is a lesson that has been lost and that this volume attempts to resurrect.

This book defends a style of feminism I call "freedom feminism." Freedom feminism stands for the moral, social, and legal equality of the sexes—and the freedom of women to employ their equal status

FREEDOM FEMINISM

> *Contemporary synthesis of egalitarian and maternal feminism*
> *Stands for the moral, social, and legal equality of the sexes*
> *Affirms for women what it affirms for everyone: dignity, fairness, and liberty*
> *Opposes efforts to impose on women (or men) stereotypical social roles, yet recognizes that men and women will typically employ their equal freedoms in distinctive ways*
> *Asserts that efforts to obliterate gender roles can be just as intolerant as efforts to maintain them*
> *Establishes that differences between the sexes, under conditions of freedom, can be a sign of social well-being. Freedom feminism is at peace, not at war, with abiding human aspiration*

to pursue happiness in their own distinctive ways. Freedom feminism is not at war with femininity or masculinity, it does not seek to bring down capitalism, and it does not view men and women as warring tribes. Conspiracy theories about universal patriarchal oppression are nowhere in its founding documents. Nor are rigid political litmus tests: it welcomes women and men from across the political spectrum. Put simply, freedom feminism affirms for women what it affirms for everyone: dignity, fairness, and liberty.

Freedom feminism is a contemporary synthesis of the two philosophies that, as we will see in chapter one, animated the feminist movement during its formative period in the eighteenth and nineteenth centuries—a radical "egalitarian school" and a conservative "maternal school." The radicals still have an important role to play today. But history has shown that for women to move forward in this world, winning broad support and respect as they go, moderate and conservative women must be at the helm. Today, moderates and conservatives need to reassert the leadership that their numbers justify. And if liberal and radical feminists want to build on the victories they have helped win, they are going to have to seek and accept assistance. For inspiration on both sides, let us look back at the glory days of the struggle for women's emancipation—not as it is often taught in feminist classrooms, but as it truly was.

1

FEMINIST FOREMOTHERS: THE EIGHTEENTH AND NINETEENTH CENTURIES

Feminism originated in the eighteenth century European Enlightenment amid the growth of a self-reliant middle class.[10] Philosophers of that age—most notably Voltaire in France and John Locke in England—celebrated the ideals of dignity, equality, and liberty for all. The growing realization that "all" included women sparked two distinct schools of thought and activism. Egalitarian feminism was progressive, individualistic, and, in the view of many contemporaries of both sexes, radical. It regarded women as independent agents rather than wives and mothers, and aimed to liberate them through appeals to universal rights. Many of today's self-described feminists are heirs to this tradition, although (as we shall see) some of their more outré views place them at the radical fringe.

Maternal feminism, by contrast, was traditionalist and family-centered. It embraced rather than rejected women's established roles as homemakers, caregivers, and providers of domestic tranquility. It promoted women's rights by redefining, strengthening, and expanding these familial roles. The maternal feminists argued that a practical, responsible, educated femininity could be a force for good beyond the family, through charitable works and more enlightened social policies.

Of the two schools, maternal feminism was far

TWO SCHOOLS OF FEMINIST THOUGHT AND ACTIVISM

EGALITARIAN FEMINISM

> *Men and women are essentially identical*

> *Secular, universalist, progressive*

> *Appealed to abstract rights and social justice*

> *Rarely achieved mainstream following*

MATERNAL FEMINISM

> *Men and women are different but equal*

> *Traditionalist, religious, and family-centered*

> *Sought to strengthen and expand women's traditional roles*

> *More popular and politically influential*

more popular and influential. Unlike its radical sister, maternal feminism has always had great appeal to the majority of women. It is not, however, my purpose to denigrate the egalitarians—quite the contrary. Historically, proponents of the two schools were sometimes fierce competitors, but their competition sharpened the arguments on both sides, and they often cooperated to great effect. The two movements were (and will remain) rivals in principle but complements in practice. Thanks to both modes of feminism, Western women now have the same rights and opportunities as men. But, as maternal feminists have always insisted, free women seldom aspire to be just like men; rather, they employ their freedom in distinctive ways and for distinctive purposes.

If feminism is to remain relevant today and earn wide allegiance in the West and in the developing world, it must reconcile with its lost sister—maternal feminism. A brief look at the lives of foremothers from both traditions will remind us what we have lost and how much could be gained by a revival of maternal feminism.

MARY WOLLSTONECRAFT: THE FIRST FEMINIST PHILOSOPHER

Egalitarian feminism had its beginnings in the writings of British philosopher Mary Wollstonecraft (1759–1797). A rebel and revolutionary thinker, Wollstonecraft believed that women were as intelligent as men and as worthy of respect. Her manifesto, *A Vindication of the Rights of Woman*, published in 1792, became an instant sensation. She wrote it in the spirit of the European Enlightenment, whose primary principle was the essential dignity and moral equality of all rational beings. In Wollstonecraft's time, her insistence that women are rational and deserving of the same rights as men was a contentious thesis.

Wollstonecraft's demand was a dramatic break with the past. In 1776, Abigail Adams famously wrote to her husband, John, urging him and his colleagues in the Continental Congress to "remember the ladies, and be more generous and favorable to them than your ancestors."[11] She was appealing to a tradition of chivalry and gallantry that enjoined male protectiveness toward women. Sixteen years later, in her *Vindication*, Wollstonecraft was doing something markedly different. She was not urging legislators in France and England to "remember the ladies" or appealing to their generous or protective impulses. Reason, she said, demanded that women possess the same rights as men. She wanted nothing less than total political and moral equality. Wollstonecraft was perhaps the first woman in history to insist that biology is not destiny: "I view, with indignation, the mistaken notions that enslave my sex."[12]

Wollstonecraft, like most political radicals of her time, was a great admirer of the French philosopher Jean-Jacques Rousseau. But she was appalled by his benighted views on women. Rousseau, an iconoclastic, original, and volatile thinker, had railed against corruption, cruelty, injustice, and unreason in the church, in the aristocracy, and in government. He had not hesitated to sweep aside centuries of traditional philosophy and religion. But, his iconoclasm did not extend to women. This philosopher who wrote in *The Social Contract*, "Man is born free; and everywhere he is in chains" was altogether untroubled by the subordination of women.

According to Rousseau, "Woman is specially made for man's delight." Women, he explained, were not merely different from men—but inferior. Their essential virtue was "docility," their proper role, "subservience." Rousseau had quipped that if women were to become like men, they would lose their power over men. Wollstonecraft coolly replied: "I don't wish them to have power over men, but over themselves."

For Wollstonecraft, education was the key to female liberation, "Strengthen the female mind by enlarging it, and there will be an end to blind obedience." She was a proponent of co-education and insisted that women be educated on a par with men—with all fields and disciplines open to them. In the opening lines of *Vindication*, she expresses her "profound conviction that the neglected education of [women] is the grand source of the misery I deplore."

Wollstonecraft led one of the most daring and

dramatic lives of the eighteenth century. She was a lower—middle-class, semi-educated "nobody" (as one British historian has described her) who became the first woman to enter the Western canon of political philosophy.[13] Her friends included Thomas Paine, William Wordsworth, and William Blake. She carried on a famous debate with the conservative political philosopher Edmund Burke about the merits of the French Revolution. Soon after she published *Vindication*, she moved to Paris to write about the revolution.

Wollstonecraft was a restless, controversial figure. After her death at the age of thirty-eight, her husband, the radical philosopher William Godwin, wrote what he thought was an adulatory biography. He talked honestly about her unorthodox lifestyle that included love affairs and an out-of-wedlock child. He even praised her—completely inaccurately—for having rejected religion on her deathbed. The public reacted to Godwin's disclosures with fascination and horror. Former friends denounced her; feminists distanced themselves; enemies gloried in her disgrace.

But by the early twentieth century, Wollstonecraft's reputation had recovered and her position as a path-breaking intellectual and reformer was secure. In an essay published in 1932, Virginia Woolf wrote, "One form of immortality

FEMINIST FOREMOTHERS

MARY WOLLSTONECRAFT (1759–1797)
EGALITARIAN FEMINIST

British writer, educator
Political philosopher
First woman to enter the Western
philosophical canon

PUBLISHED
"A Vindication of the Rights
of Woman" (1792)

KEY CONTRIBUTIONS
Women are as intelligent and rational
as men and worthy of equal rights.

is hers undoubtedly: she is alive and active, she argues and experiments, we hear her voice and trace her influence even now among the living." Woolf praised the book as "so true" that it "seems to contain nothing new." Its originality, she said, "has become our commonplace."[14]

In the early 1990s, more than 200 years after the publication of Wollstonecraft's *Vindication*, Somali-born Dutch dissident Ayaan Hirsi Ali found herself struggling to discover ways to assert the rights of Muslim women. The contemporary feminist theory that she read made little sense to her; it seemed irrelevant to the plight of women tyrannized by political Islam. But after a copy of *Vindication* fell into her hands, Hirsi Ali writes of being "inspired by Mary Wollstonecraft, the pioneering feminist thinker who told women they had the same ability to reason as men did and deserved the same rights."[15] Wollstonecraft has not been forgotten; she survives in history, and young women such as Hirsi Ali find her powerful and inspiring.

HANNAH MORE AND THE BLUESTOCKINGS

At the time Wollstonecraft was writing, the longer-lived Hannah More (1745–1833)—a novelist, poet, pamphleteer, political activist, evangelical reformer, and abolitionist—was waging a very different campaign to improve the status of women. More is well known to scholars of eighteenth-century culture. The late UCLA literary historian Mitzi Myers called her a "female crusader infinitely more successful than Wollstonecraft or any other competitor."[16] But More is rarely given the credit she deserves. I describe her philosophy and work in

FEMINIST FOREMOTHERS

HANNAH MORE (1745–1833)
MATERNAL FEMINIST

Novelist, poet, pamphleteer
Political activist
Evangelical Christian, abolitionist
Known as "the first Victorian"
* and "Christian capitalist"*
Member of Bluestocking circle

PUBLISHED
"Strictures on the Modern System
of Female Education" (1799)

KEY CONTRIBUTIONS
Empowered femininity: women should
educate and exert themselves "with a
patriotism at once firm and feminine,
for the greater good of all."

some detail because this extraordinary woman has
been left out of the feminist canon.

If Wollstonecraft is the founder of egalitarian

feminism, More is the founder of maternal feminism. More was a religiously inspired, self-made woman who became an intellectual peer of several of the most accomplished men of her age. But where Wollstonecraft had befriended Thomas Paine and debated Edmund Burke, More was a friend and admirer of Burke, a close friend of Samuel Johnson and Horace Walpole, and an indispensable ally and confidante to William Wilberforce, a father of British abolitionism. Concerning the French Revolution, which Wollstonecraft initially championed, More wrote, "From liberty, equality, and the rights of man, good Lord deliver us."[17]

And she was surely the most prominent woman of her age. As one biographer notes, "In her time she was better known than Mary Wollstonecraft and her books outsold Jane Austen's many times over."[18] According to one literary historian, nineteenth century Americans were more familiar with the writings of Hannah More than the plays of Shakespeare.[19] More's various pamphlets sold in the millions, and her tract against the French Revolution enjoyed a greater circulation than Burke's *Reflections on the Revolution in France* or Paine's *Rights of Man*.

More, who never married, was active in the Bluestocking circle, a group of intellectual women and men who would meet to discuss politics, literature, science, and philosophy. The group was founded in 1750 by intelligent but education-starved upper- and middle-class women who yearned for serious conversation rather than the chatter and gossip typical of elite gatherings. "I, a girl, was educated at random,"[20] More would say, and women's education became one of her most passionate causes.

More is hard to classify politically. It is possible to find passages in her novels, pamphlets, and letters that make her sound like an anti-feminist; others show her as a progressive reformer and visionary women's advocate. Through selective citation, she can be made to seem like an insufferable prude; Lord Byron dismissed her as "Morality's prim personification."[21] But it is doubtful that such a "prim personification" would have attracted the respect and devotion of men such as Johnson, Walpole, and Wilberforce.

More was a British patriot and a champion of constitutional monarchy, and an admirer of Burke, but she was no defender of the status quo. Writing at the height of the Evangelical Revival, she was one of those calling for revolutionary change—not in politics, but in morals. In her novels and pamphlets, she sharply reproached members of the upper classes for their amorality, hedonism, indifference to the poor, and tolerance of the crime of slavery. (She urged housewives to boycott West Indian sugar, which abolitionists described as "steeped in the blood of our fellow creatures."[22]) In the many Sunday schools she established, poor children were taught to read and encouraged to be sober, thrifty, hardworking, and religious. In her writings, she promoted the same virtues for the wealthy. More shared Adam Smith's enthusiasm for the free market as a force for good. But for the market to thrive, she believed England's poor and rich would need to develop good moral habits and virtuous characters.

Historians have referred to More as a "bourgeois progressivist," a "Christian capitalist," "Burke for beginners," and the "first Victorian," but she was also the first maternal feminist. Unlike Wollstonecraft, she believed the sexes were significantly different in their propensities, aptitudes, and preferences, but she was a great proponent of empowered femininity. She envisioned a society in which women's characteristic virtues and graces could be developed, refined, and freely expressed. She was persuaded that these virtues could be realized only when women were given more freedom and a serious education. As she wrote in *Strictures on the Modern System of Female Education* (1799),

> [T]ill women shall be more reasonably educated, and until the native growth of their mind shall cease to be stinted and

cramped, we shall have no juster ground for pronouncing that their understanding has already reached its highest attainable perfection, than the Chinese would have for affirming that their women have attained to the greatest possible perfection in walking, while their first care is, during their infancy, to cripple their feet.[23]

She loathed the mindless pastimes that absorbed upper-class women of her day and encouraged middle- and upper-class women to leave their homes and salons to take up serious philanthropic pursuits. Why, asked More, should women settle for being "captivating for a day" when they possessed the power for actions whose "effects may be commensurate with eternity."[24] According to More, women were more tender-minded than men and were the natural caretakers of the nation. She told women that it was their patriotic duty to apply their natural gifts—nurturing, organizing, and educating—not merely to their own households, but to society at large. "Charity," said a character in one of More's novels, "is the calling of a lady; the care of the poor is her profession."[25] More envisioned armies of intelligent, informed, and well-trained "domestic heroines" working in hospitals, orphanages, and schools. She appealed to women to exert themselves "with a patriotism at once firm and feminine, for the greater good of all."[26]

Her didactic 1809 novel, *Coelebs in Search of a Wife*, which valorized a new kind of wise, effective, and active femininity, was so popular that it went through eleven editions in nine months and thirty by the time of her death. UCLA literary scholar Anne Mellor comments on More's influence:

> She urged her women readers to work aggressively in the organization of voluntary benevolent societies and in the foundation of hospitals, orphanages, Sunday Schools. . . . And her call was heard: literally thousands of voluntary societies sprang up in the opening decades of the nineteenth century to serve the needs of every imaginable group of sufferers.[27]

It is hard to overstate the positive impact on the fate of women of the widespread volunteerism preached by More. When women engaged in charitable works, other parts of the public sphere became accessible. Women galvanized by More's call for good works later played a prominent role in the movement for women's suffrage.[28]

It was taken for granted in More's time that women were less intelligent, less serious, and less important than men. More adamantly rejected these assumptions. She did so, however, without rejecting the idea of a special women's sphere. She embraced that sphere and looked for ways to give it greater dignity and power. That was her signature style of conservative feminism. More initiated a humane revolution in the relations of the sexes that was decorous, civilized, and socially cohesive. Above all, it was a feminism that women themselves could comfortably embrace: a feminism that empowered and freed women on their terms. Indeed, if More's name and fame had not been airbrushed out of contemporary women's history, many today might identify with a modernized version of her female-friendly feminism.

Fortunately, her ideals and her style of feminism are well represented in the novels of Jane Austen. Scholars claim to see the influence of both More and Wollstonecraft in Austen's writings. Her heroines are paragons of rational, merciful, and responsible womanhood. Austen also honors a style of enlightened and chivalrous manhood. Austen's heroes—men like Mr. Darcy, Captain Wentworth, and Mr. Knightley—esteem female strength, rationality, and intelligence.

Egalitarian feminists like Wollstonecraft (and later John Stuart Mill and Harriet Taylor) are enshrined in the present-day canon of feminists, but they never attracted a very large following among the rank and file of women of their time. By contrast, More succeeded brilliantly with all classes of women. She awakened a nation and changed the way it saw itself. Her achievements were unprecedented. So, it is unfortunate that her historical significance as the great popularizer of maternal feminism is largely unrecognized.

Anne Mellor, the UCLA literary scholar asks: "Why has Hannah More been so relentlessly condemned by, even on occasion erased from, the most widely read historical accounts . . . ?"[29] Her answer (which she admits is speculative) is that many of the leading scholars who specialize on the eighteenth and nineteenth century are committed to "left-wing social ideologies." Because of this, says Mellor, "They *hate* Hannah More because in their eyes she did far too much to stop a liberating-French style of political revolution occurring in England" (emphasis in original).[30] Hate is the right word. The influential Marxist social historian E. P. Thompson accused More of fear mongering and brainwashing the working class. In one memorable 1975 attack, another radical historian calls her a "necrophiliac . . . opportunist."[31] Feminist academics have joined the fray. Literary scholar Elizabeth Kowaleski-Wallace speaks for many of her sister theorists when she describes More as a case study of "patriarchal complicity" and an "uninvited guest" who "make[s] the process of celebrating our heritage as women more difficult."[32]

But "our heritage"—if that means the full story of female emancipation—was made by conservative as well as egalitarian women. Together these two branches of feminism helped liberate women from the narrow spheres that confined them. The complementarity of Wollstonecraft and More was vital to the progress of women in the eighteenth century. It remains vital today. Wollstonecraft's demand for full equality continues to inspire, but so does More's notion of effective femininity. Many contemporary women in both the developed and developing world want their rights and freedoms, but they still want to give priority to their roles as wives and mothers. They continue to prevail in the helping and caring domains celebrated by More. Her vision of domestic heroism still has the power to inspire millions of women.

FRANCES WILLARD: "SAINT FRANCES OF AMERICAN WOMANHOOD"

Hannah More is not the only once-famous women's advocate to have vanished from the women's pantheon. Ken Burns, the celebrated documentarian, followed his award-winning *The Civil War* with a 1999 film about Elizabeth Cady Stanton

FEMINIST FOREMOTHERS

ELIZABETH CADY STANTON (1815–1902)
SUSAN B. ANTHONY (1820–1906)
EGALITARIAN SUFFRAGIST LEADERS
AND FIRST-WAVE FEMINISTS

Writers, speakers
Abolitionists

KEY CONTRIBUTIONS
Promoted women's suffrage and other
rights through appeals to universal
rights. They defended, in Stanton's
words, "the individuality of each
human soul" and a woman's need to be
"arbiter of her own destiny."

(1815–1902) and Susan B. Anthony (1820–1906) and their struggle to win the vote for American women.[33] In one brief sequence, the narrator explains that in the last quarter of the nineteenth century, Anthony forged coalitions with conservative mainstream groups. The mood darkens, and Sally Roesch Wagner, a pioneer in the field of women's studies, appears on the screen. Wagner informs viewers that Anthony was so determined to win the vote that she established alliances with pro-suffrage women who were "enemies of freedom in every other way—Frances Willard is a case in point." The camera moves to a photo of a dour-looking Willard.

One would never imagine from Burns' film that Willard (1839–1898) was one of the most beloved and respected women of the nineteenth century. When she died, one newspaper wrote, "No woman's name is better known in the English speaking world than that of Miss Willard, save that of England's great queen."[34] Because of her prodigious good works and kindness, Willard was often called the "Saint Frances of American Womanhood."

Willard served as president of the Woman's Christian Temperance Union (WCTU) from 1879 until her death in 1898. Today we think of the temperance crusaders as grim-faced scolds—Carrie Nation, the six-foot-tall, hatchet-wielding saloon wrecker comes to mind. But, under Willard's inspired leadership, the WCTU developed into a powerful and effective movement that promoted causes as diverse as prison reform, child welfare, and care for the disabled in addition to suffrage and temperance. Though largely a white, middle-class organization, the WCTU attracted considerable numbers of Native American, immigrant, and

FEMINIST FOREMOTHERS

FRANCES WILLARD (1839–1898)
MATERNAL FEMINIST

Educator
Known as "Saint Frances of
  American Womanhood"
President of the Women's Christian
  Temperance Union

KEY CONTRIBUTIONS
With the vote, women could greatly
increase their humane and civilizing
influence on society. She viewed
"womanliness" as a virtue and
described her philanthropic
organization as being "of the women,
by the women, but for humanity."

black women. According to one study, 30 percent of its local leaders were wives of skilled or unskilled workers.[35] Most late-nineteenth-century social reformers, including Stanton, Anthony, and Sojourner Truth, supported the ban of alcohol.

They believed that banning its sale would greatly diminish wife abuse, desertion, destitution, and crime. Temperance was a movement in defense of the female sphere: the saloon was the enemy of the home.

Feminist founders like Stanton and Anthony promoted women's suffrage through appeals to universal rights. Their inspirations were John Locke, Thomas Paine, and Thomas Jefferson. Stanton admired Hannah More, whom she called "one of the great minds of her day," but Stanton's own style of feminism was in the egalitarian tradition of Mary Wollstonecraft.[36] Stanton wrote affectingly on "the individuality of each human soul" and on a woman's need to be the "arbiter of her own destiny."[37] She and her sister egalitarians brought an Enlightenment feminism to women, but to their abiding disappointment, American women greeted the offer with a mixture of indifference and hostility. Stanton's inspiring words resonated with a relatively small coterie of educated women, mostly in the East. When a suffrage amendment failed dismally in the state of Colorado in 1877, one newspaper editorial called the suffragists "carpetbaggers" promoting an elitist "eastern issue." The headline read: "Good-bye to the Female Tramps of Boston."[38]

It is the conventional wisdom that men denied women the ballot. But even a cursory look at the historical record shows that men were not the only problem. In 1895, Massachusetts held a referendum on women's suffrage: both men and women were allowed to vote. The initiative lost, with 187,000 voting against the franchise and 110,000 in favor—and of those who voted yes, only 23,000 were women.[39] Suffragists protested that the referendum was a little more than a stunt contrived by anti-suffrage forces. But why, given the opportunity, didn't women flock to the polls in support of their right to vote?

Anthony and her co-author offered an answer in their 1902 history of women's suffrage: "In the indifference, the inertia, the apathy of women lies the greatest obstacle to their enfranchisement."[40] According to Anthony, "The average man would not vote against granting women the franchise if all those of his own family and the circle of his intimate friends brought a strong pressure to bear upon him in its favor."[41] For many decades, most American women simply ignored the cause of suffrage—or actively opposed it. Stanford historian Carl Degler, in his classic 1980 social history, *At Odds: Women and the Family in America from the Revolution to the Present*, notes that by the 1890s, more than twenty thousand women had joined an anti-suffrage group in New York State alone.[42]

Degler and other historians believe that because

the vote was associated with individualism and personal assertiveness, many women saw it as selfish and an attack on their unique and valued place in the family. Some feminist historians denigrate what they call the "cult of domesticity" that proved so beguiling to nineteenth-century women. But they forget that this "cult" freed many rural women from manual labor, improved the material conditions of women's lives, and coincided with an increase in female life expectancy. Furthermore, as Degler shows, in nineteenth-century America both the public and private spheres were prized and valued. The companionate marriages described by Jane Austen were the American domestic ideal. Alexis de Tocqueville commented on the essential equality of the male and female spheres in *Democracy in America* (1840). Americans, he said, did not think that men and women should perform the same tasks, "but they show an equal regard for both their respective parts; and though their lot is different, they consider both of them as being of equal value."[43]

Hence, as long as women remained indifferent or hostile, suffrage was a lost cause. Impassioned feminist rhetoric about freedom, dignity, autonomy, and individual rights fell on deaf ears. If the American women's movement was going to move forward, it needed new arguments and new ways of thinking that were more respectful and protective of women's role. Frances Willard showed the way.

Willard was proud of the woman's role as the "angel in the house." But why, she asked, limit these angels to the home? "Of the women, by the women, but for humanity" was Willard's motto for her organization. And that motto resonated with women from every sector of American life. The WCTU provided thousands of traditional, non-political women their first experience with public activism. They learned how to work with other women, assume leadership positions, and organize around pressing social causes. Along the way, they became receptive to Willard's idea that voting was a woman's sacred duty. With the vote, Willard said, women could greatly increase their humane and civilizing influence on society. With the vote, they could protect the homes they so dearly loved—indeed, she referred to the vote as "the home protection ballot."[44] Women were galvanized by Willard's vision of an elevated femininity; men were disarmed. The late historian Ruth Bordin has called the WCTU "one of the most powerful instruments of women's consciousness-raising of all time."[45]

Susan B. Anthony admired Willard; Elizabeth Cady Stanton, a religious skeptic, was leery. Both were startled by Willard's ability to attract unprecedented numbers of dedicated women to the suffrage cause. In 1890, two leading egalitarian suffragist groups merged because they were worried that the cause was dying. They formed the National American Woman Suffrage Association and elected Stanton president. The new groups claimed 13,000 members, but as Anthony said in an 1893 speech, "I will tell you frankly and honestly that all we number is seven thousand."[46] By comparison, Willard had built an organization with 150,000 dues-paying members, along with an additional 50,000 in branches for young women.[47]

Willard and her followers brought the suffrage movement something new and unfamiliar: electoral victories. In 1893, the state of Colorado held a second referendum on women's suffrage. Unlike 1877, when the suffragists lost and the so-called "tramps of Boston" were sent packing, this time the suffragists won with 55 percent. In a close analysis of their referendum victory, historian Suzanne Marilley shows how Colorado suffragists made use of Willard's network as well as her traditionalist "home-protection" philosophy. "Willard's arguments," says Marilley, "had to have dampened the virulent opposition that had defeated the measure in 1877."[48]

When Willard died in 1898, her younger feminist colleague Carrie Chapman Catt remarked, "There has never been a woman leader in this country greater than nor perhaps so great as Frances

Willard."[49] It would take another twenty-two years of political mobilization before the Nineteenth Amendment, ratified in 1920, guaranteed women the vote in all state and federal elections, but thanks to Willard millions of women and men were ready to sign on to that cause. Willard's WCTU and its maternal feminist philosophy inspired a new consensus. As Ruth Bordin says, "With its tens of thousands of members it did provide the mass base from which twentieth-century suffrage movement could take off."[50]

Today's women's movement keeps its distance from Willard's notion of feminine virtue and has little sympathy with her family-centered philosophy. But these are precisely the traits that make Willard's feminism so relevant to the women across the developing world who are struggling for their rights but who do not want to be "liberated" from the roles of wife and mother.

In her 1990 book, *In Search of Islamic Feminism*, the late Elizabeth Warnock Fernea, a University of Texas Middle Eastern studies professor, described a new style of feminism coming to life in the Muslim world. Traveling through Uzbekistan, Saudi Arabia, Morocco, Turkey, and Iraq, Fernea met great numbers of women's advocates working to improve the status of women. There have always been Western-style egalitarian feminists in these countries, but they are few and tend to be found among the educated elites. The "Islamic feminists" Fernea met were different. They were traditional, religious, and family-centered—and they had a following among women from all social classes. They were proud of women's roles as mothers, wives, and caregivers. Several rejected what they saw as divisiveness in the American women's movement. As one Iraqi women's advocate, Haifa Abdul Rahman, told her, "We see feminism in America as dividing women from men—separating women from the family. This is not good for anyone."[51]

Fernea settled on the term "family feminism" to describe this new movement. Historians of Western feminism will recognize the affinities with Willard's long-lost teachings. Today, almost twenty years after Fernea's book, maternal feminism is surging in the Muslim world.[52] Truth be told, great numbers of contemporary American women would also readily embrace feminism were they aware of an alternative that respects the domestic sphere.

Thomas Carlyle once ascribed the insights of genius to "cooperation with the real tendency of the world."[53] Like Hannah More before her, Frances Willard cooperated with the world and discerned novel and effective ways to improve social arrangements. Though few today know who these women were, their ideas are still with us. Indeed, those ideas are demonstrating their power anew in today's most urgent battleground for women's rights.

2

**THE SECOND WAVE:
SINCE 1960**

THE GREAT CONVERGENCE

The uneasy alliances between radical and conservative feminists in the eighteenth and nineteenth centuries led to momentous improvements in the social status and everyday lives of women. In *Two Paths to Women's Equality* (1995), Brandeis University scholar Janet Zollinger Giele tells how American women won suffrage only when egalitarian groups led by Elizabeth Cady Stanton and Susan B. Anthony formed a coalition with moderate mainstream women led by Frances Willard. Says Giele, "History records defeat in every instance where one branch failed to recognize the valid arguments of the other."[54] When the two branches cooperated, success followed.

The efforts that culminated in the Nineteenth Amendment made up the "first wave" of feminism. Then, forty years after American women won the vote in the early twentieth century, history repeated itself in what is known as the "second wave" of feminism. Once again, the combined efforts of egalitarians and traditionalists achieved what neither could have done alone—extending women's rights from the ballot box to the courts, the workplace, the university, and beyond.

According to popular wisdom, the great victories of second-wave women's liberation were won by bra-burning, street-protesting radicals in the late 1960s and 1970s. Two things are wrong with this standard view. First, no bras were ever burned (though a few girdles may have been thrown into a "freedom trash can"). More important, the second wave actually began in the early 1960s and was moved by a coalition of Republican and Democratic women (and men). The radicals came later—after several landmark victories had been won.

The achievement of full women's suffrage in the United States was followed by a long hiatus in further steps toward legal equality. Americans had other priorities—the exuberance of the Roaring Twenties, the Depression of the 1930s, and World War II in the 1940s. When Americans returned to the pursuit of the American Dream in the late 1940s, the country was ready for an egalitarian adjustment. Attitudes had changed, as had women's aspirations. Women had contributed valiantly to the war effort abroad and war production at home. They had entered the workforce in unprecedented numbers, often performing hard and arduous work. These experiences left many thinking that, at least in the workplace, the unequal treatment of women was anachronistic and unjust.

The women's movement had never completely gone away. It had remained an important component of the labor movement, dominated by maternal feminists who focused on workplace protections for women and children. But now employment equality was becoming a consensus issue, and both conservatives and liberals, Republicans and Democrats, were in the forefront. Gallup surveys show that 76 percent of the population supported equal pay for equal work as early as 1945, up to 87 percent by 1954.[55] In Congress, the Equal Pay Act was introduced in the late 1940s by Robert Taft, Republican senator from Ohio, and Claude Pepper, Democratic representative from Florida.[54] By 1960, dozens of bills against sex discrimination were in the congressional hopper with bipartisan sponsorship.

Basic employment laws were enacted in the early 1960s. The reformers were a group of Republican and Democratic female lawyers, commissioners, and legislators—mostly in pearls and high heels. These women, aided by male colleagues, persuaded Congress to pass the Equal Pay Act in 1963, which made it illegal to pay men and women different salaries for the same work. Because of their efforts, the landmark Civil Rights Act of 1964 included a provision, Title VII, prohibiting sex discrimination in hiring and promotion.

These enactments were, in retrospect, the decisive first steps in second-wave feminism and the achievement of full legal equality for women; there would be no turning back. But they were general policies, and they applied primarily to employment. It would take many years of enforcement, interpretation, and social assimilation before the policies were realized in practice. And there were many more issues to be addressed, especially equality in education, family law, and property law. For the time being, women remained second-class citizens. Those who preferred paths other than wife and mother, and those who found the stereotypes of femininity stultifying, remained limited in their opportunities for fulfillment.

These frustrations found a powerful voice in Betty Friedan's bestselling 1963 manifesto, *The Feminine Mystique*. In 1966, Friedan and her colleagues founded the National Organization for Women (NOW) to eliminate discrimination against women. Initially, its membership included a contingent of political women of both parties who had been part of the efforts to pass the Equal Pay Act and Title VII. But NOW quickly attracted a more diverse group of followers, including housewives who were galvanized by Friedan's book as well as radical younger women who came from the anti-war movement. It was an uneasy alliance, but it worked—initially. The three groups cooperated to advance the cause of women at a time when the country was highly amenable to change.

University of Minnesota historian Sara Evans calls the years between 1968 and 1975 feminism's "golden years." According to Evans, "the U.S.

Congress seemed hell-bent on figuring out just what women wanted and giving it to them. Hearings, votes, and legislative victories came with breathtaking speed."[57] In 1972, for example, Congress passed the Title IX equity law that granted women equal rights in education and the Equal Employment Opportunity Act that expanded the scope and strengthened the enforcement of Title VII of the Civil Rights Act. The laws were supported and signed by Richard Nixon, a socially conservative Republican.

At the same time, courts were busy striking down one discriminatory state law after another. The Supreme Court, at the time all-male and Republican dominated, ruled that husbands could no longer hold complete control of community property (1971);[58] that women could not be denied

---

EQUAL RIGHTS AMENDMENT (ERA)

SECTION 1. *Equality of rights under the law shall not be denied or abridged by the United States or by any state on account of sex.*

---

employment because they had children (1971);[59] that servicewomen as well as servicemen could claim their spouses as dependents (1973);[60] that employers could not force pregnant women into mandatory maternity leave (1974);[61] and that states could not have different rules for men and women concerning jury duty (1975).[62]

What was happening in Congress and in the courts during the "golden years" reflected popular sentiment and led to a momentous further step. A coalition of conservatives, liberals, and radicals converged around the idea of amending the U.S. Constitution to guarantee women full equality with men. The proposed Equal Rights Amendment (ERA), first introduced to Congress in 1923, read simply: "Equality of rights under the law shall not be denied or abridged by the United States or by any state on account of sex."[63] It had languished in congressional committees for fifty years. But by 1970, success was imminent. Or so it seemed.

THE RISE AND FALL OF THE ERA

In the beginning, Republican leaders were as enthusiastic about the ERA as their Democratic counterparts, if not more so. Presidents Eisenhower, Nixon, and Ford endorsed it. After it passed the House in 1971 by a nearly unanimous vote, it momentarily stalled in the Senate thanks to the objections of a powerful Democratic senator from North Carolina, Sam Ervin. Said Ervin, "Keep the law responsible where the good Lord put it—on the man to bear the burdens of support and on the women to bear the children." Ervin's sentiments did not resonate widely at a time when Helen Reddy's feminist anthem, "I Am Woman. Hear Me Roar," was at the top of the pop music charts. Ervin's opposition to what he called the "Equal Wrongs Amendment" was no match for the burgeoning national network of pro-ERA activists. As one activist remembers, "It got so you could make twelve phone calls and [generate] five to ten thousand letters."[64] On March 22, 1972, by a vote of 84 to 8, the Senate passed the ERA.

The legislature of Hawaii, eager for the honor of making theirs the first state in the union to ratify the historic amendment, gave its unanimous support twenty minutes after the Senate vote. Within days, the legislatures of Delaware, New Hampshire, Nebraska, Iowa, and Idaho all voted unanimously for the amendment. Dozens more followed in the next few years. Not a single governor opposed the ERA. Newspapers and magazines were excited supporters, including the traditionalist *Redbook, Family Circle, Good Housekeeping*, and *Parenting*.

The ERA did have its critics. The *New York Times* ran an editorial in 1972, entitled "The Henpecked

House," criticizing the amendment's "mischievous ambiguity."[65] *Times* columnist James J. Kilpatrick described the ERA as a "contrivance of a gang of professional harpies"; male legislators voted for it with one purpose in mind, he said—"Get these furies off their backs."[66] But such carping counted for little compared with the overwhelming political support and ecstatic endorsements from celebrities such as Carol Burnett, Lily Tomlin, Paul Newman, Lauren Bacall, Candice Bergen, and Ann Landers. Ratification seemed inevitable.

THE FORMIDABLE MRS. SCHLAFLY

Most historians agree that the ERA would have passed had it not been for the efforts of a single woman—Phyllis Schlafly of Alton, Illinois. Schlafly came from a hard-scrabble Depression-era family but managed to find her way into Washington University in St. Louis, where she graduated in 1944 with honors. She paid her way through college by working a forty-eight-hour-a-week night shift at a munitions factory where she test-fired rifles and machine guns to measure their speed and accuracy. Later, she earned a master's degree in political science from Radcliffe and then, in middle age, a law degree. By the 1960s, she had become a nationally known advocate for political conservatism as well as a wife and mother of six. A conservative Catholic, she called politics her "hobby," but it was a hobby that included running for Congress twice (the first time when she was 26 with a toddler in tow), making more than 100 annual public appearances, and writing books, including the 1964 bestseller about Barry Goldwater, *A Choice Not an Echo*. She worked for a time at the American Enterprise Institute in Washington and became a specialist in strategic nuclear policy. As one reluctantly admiring feminist leader would say, "I just can't think of anyone who's so together and tough. I mean, [she is] everything you should raise your daughter to be. . . . She's an extremely liberated woman."[67]

Schlafly became an anti–ERA activist by accident. In December 1971, she was invited to speak at a bookstore in Connecticut. "OK," she said, "I will talk on strategic balance."[68] When the host urged her to address the ERA, she explained that she knew little about the amendment and wasn't even sure what side she was on. Her host sent her a packet of materials. When she read them, she had a "click" experience—the term feminists use to describe that dazzling moment of realization when a woman first apprehends how oppressed she is. But in Schlafly's case, the click was a dazzling realization of how destructive the ERA would be were it ever to pass.

Critics falsely accused her of making common cause with the Ku Klux Klan and the ultra-right-wing John Birch Society. In fact, her inspiration came from her own careful reading of feminist literature as well as legal critiques of the ERA by prominent constitutional scholars such as Philip Kurland of the University of Chicago Law School and Paul Freund of the Harvard Law School. Said Freund, for example,

> I am in wholehearted sympathy with the efforts to remove . . . vestigial laws that work an injustice to women. . . . However, not every legal differential between boys and girls, men and women, husbands and wives, is of this obnoxious character, and to compress . . . [them] into one tight little formula is to invite confusion, anomaly, and dismay.[69]

As Schlafly would explain in detail in talks and debates, by 1972 most of the laws that had treated men and women differently had already been stricken from the books. She would often praise the Equal Pay Act, Title VII of the Civil Rights Act, and the early court victories. She readily conceded that she had benefited from these reforms. Nor was she opposed to women having careers: she had a brilliant one herself. But through her reading she had become convinced that the ERA was not about equality of opportunity. American women were well on their way to having that. So what was it about?

In a recent history of second-wave feminism, *When Everything Changed*, *New York Times* writer Gail Collins confirms Schlafly's argument that the goals of the ERA had already been achieved. According to Collins, "[B]y the mid-70s, between the courts and the legislatures, most of the laws that the ERA was intended to vanquish had already been eliminated or neutralized."[70] Legislators were eager to pass the amendment, says Collins, because they viewed it as a gesture of goodwill toward women: it was symbolic rather than substantive.

But, as Schlafly showed, the ERA was much more than a symbol for its most ardent supporters: it was a blueprint for a radically new society. Much of the feminist literature, for example, took a dim view of women's prevalence in the domestic sphere. In *The Feminine Mystique*, Betty Friedan had called the suburban home a "comfortable concentration camp" where women suffer a "slow death of mind and spirit." Like the inmates of the camps, she said, American housewives had become "walking corpses."[71] In building her case, Friedan not only attacked a postwar culture that consigned women to the domestic sphere, but she attacked the domestic sphere itself and all the women who chose to live there. When *McCall's* magazine printed excerpts from the book, it received hundreds of letters—overwhelmingly negative. Letter writers found Friedan snobbish and condescending. "Stop knocking the homemaker," wrote one. Another: "I am a proud and fulfilled wife, mother, daughter, sister, trying to live up to my purpose of being here on earth; no small nor ignominious task I can assure you."[72] Critics would later point out Friedan's seeming indifference to poor women who "longed to be housewives," but had no choice but to work fulltime.[73] One admiring reviewer extolled *The Feminine Mystique* for having "pulled the trigger on history."[74] Schlafly saw it differently. Friedan and her sisters-in-arms might have pulled the trigger on history, but they were taking aim not only at legal and social inequality but also at the way of life of millions of American women.

Schlafly had a straightforward reply to the assault on housewives, which angered many feminists but rang true with great numbers of women. "Women's libbers"—short for advocates of women's liberation—"view the home as a prison and the wife and mother as a slave. . . . The libbers don't understand that most women want to be a wife, mother and homemaker—and are happy in that role."[75] Feminists, unaccustomed to dissent, were sometimes unhinged by her critiques. In a 1973 debate between Schlafly and Friedan over the ERA, an irate Friedan said to Schlafly, "I'd like to burn you at the stake." The unflappable Schlafly advised audience members to take note of the "intemperate nature of proponents of the ERA."[76]

In 1973, Schlafly debated an official from NOW on William F. Buckley Jr.'s television program, *Firing Line*. Buckley read the text of the ERA, "Equality of rights under the law shall not be denied or abridged . . . on account of sex." Buckley said to Schlafly what must have been on many viewers' minds: "That does not sound particularly subversive." Why would anyone want to deny women their rights?[77]

Schlafly explained that the amendment was about not women's rights, but imposing an eccentric agenda on an unsuspecting nation. She pointed out that the amendment not only denigrated housewives, but it could also be used to require state-funded abortion, as well as the elimination of all forms of so-called gender "segregation," including mother-son picnics and single-sex schools. If it passed, said Schlafly, young women would be subject to the military draft. "You have to be equal across the board, in combat—on warships, and all up and down the military line."[78]

Buckley expected the representative from NOW, Ann Scott, to dispute these claims. Schlafly's critics had accused her of misrepresenting the ERA and engaging in "alarmist apocalypticism."[79] Instead,

Scott agreed with Schlafly's predictions—but unlike Schlafly, she thought they were desirable and long overdue. "There is no question that if the ERA is passed women would become subject to the draft. . . . If women are to be citizens, and citizens are to be subject to the draft, then women should take the responsibilities as well as the rights of citizenship."[80] Buckley asked Scott if she and her colleagues at NOW would consider a compromise: allow women to volunteer for military training and combat but don't make it compulsory. Scott bristled. Failure to accord women the "difficulties that citizenship entails" is "to lower our status as human beings."[81] Even today the idea of drafting women into combat on par with men is controversial and a majority opposes it.[82] In the 1970s it was, for most Americans, unfathomable.

Schlafly was certain that members of Congress and state legislatures had not meant to ratify Betty Friedan's angry worldview or NOW's increasingly radical agenda. She saw clearly that the amendment could be used in ways never dreamed of by its congressional supporters. The goal was radical egalitarianism. No exceptions. No compromise. She was determined to blow the whistle as loud as she could.

Working with a small group of women from her kitchen in Alton, Schlafly organized one of the most successful grassroots campaigns in American history.

In a world without faxes, email, or the Internet, she made her case via the telephone, speeches, and her monthly newsletter, *The Phyllis Schlafly Report*. At her own expense, she reprinted and distributed a NOW manifesto entitled *Revolution: Tomorrow Is NOW* so readers could learn what the organization stood for in its own words. Among the revolution's targets? Women's penchant for charitable work and community service: "Volunteering is yet another form of activity which serves to reinforce the second-class status of women . . . and thus is detrimental to the liberation of women."[83] This was NOW turning against two centuries of maternal feminism.

ERA activists initially dismissed Schlafly as a crank, but they underestimated her badly. Her organizing and debating skills would become the stuff of legend. *New York Times* editor Joseph Lelyveld would write in 1977 that "Phyllis Schlafly has become one of the most relentless and accomplished platform debaters of any gender to be found on any side of any issue."[84]

Her sense of humor and flair for political theater did not hurt either. She would create havoc at meetings with feminists by first saying, "I want to thank my husband Fred for letting me come."[85] Outspent and outnumbered, Schlafly and her followers found ways to steal the ERA's thunder. During statehouse debates, little children would appear with signs saying, "Please don't send my mommy to war."[86] At a huge ERA rally in 1976, women from across the country gathered in Springfield, Illinois, to show support for what they called "The Second American Revolution." But news stories focused instead on an airplane that flew above the rally carrying a banner— "Illinois women oppose the ERA—libbers go home" (an echo of that Colorado newspaper headline in 1877). Schlafly also garnered attention sharing a podium with a preacher in a gorilla suit carrying a protest sign that read, "Don't Monkey with the Constitution."[87]

Schlafly had another big advantage—the framers had made it hard to amend the Constitution. The amendment had to be ratified by at least three-fourths of the states—thirty-eight state legislatures. The thirty-fifth ratification—Indiana's in 1977— turned out to be the last. The unheralded anti-ERA movement was making a once feel-good amendment controversial and contentious. The increasingly extreme arguments of NOW and other ERA supporters were making it even more so. When Schlafly spoke to the state legislatures, ERA enthusiasm waned. For the first time, states began to vote the amendment down—Florida, North Carolina, Oklahoma. Others tried to rescind their earlier ratification votes—Idaho, Nebraska, Kentucky, and Tennessee. The once decorous, inclusive ratification campaign turned hard, with lawsuits, boycotts of non-ratifying states, and a successful effort to extend the ratification deadline from seven to ten years.

In the spring of 1982, with the ratification deadline looming and the amendment apparently going down in defeat, NOW staged massive demonstrations and vigils and frenzied lobbying in a remaining handful of hopeful states. In Illinois, a group of women chained themselves to the doors of the State Senate chamber "to dramatize the economic slavery we are in."[88] Others smuggled in bags of pig blood and scrawled the names of anti-ERA legislators on the marble floor of the capitol. Outside, activists scorched giant letters "ERA" onto the lawn. A group leader, Sonia Johnson, organized a hunger strike in the capitol rotunda with eight other women. It lasted for 38 days before they slunk home in defeat. Some historians describe Johnson and the other militants as fringe activists. But a few months later, Johnson would run for the presidency of NOW. She lost, but managed to get 40 percent of the votes.[89]

The ERA campaign ended in the summer of 1982. Its champions had failed to garner enough votes, and the clock had run out. Schlafly's genius was to figure out as early as 1972 that the forces behind the ERA did not represent American women.

And, against all odds and with the unintended collaboration of the ERA forces, she prevailed.

Had the ERA supporters compromised—exempted women from combat, and made a few other common-sense concessions to maternal feminism—the amendment would certainly have passed. But, as historian Jane Mansbridge explains in *Why We Lost the ERA*, by the mid-seventies most feminist leaders held that "the ERA would require the military to send women draftees into combat on the same basis as men." They did so, she says "because their ideology called for full equality with men, not for equality with exceptions."[90]

As we have seen, women were already gaining equality rapidly, and what most of them wanted was an equality that allowed for differences. In the 1970s, just as today, Americans viewed many differences between women and men as natural, socially important, non-invidious, and (at least to many) the enjoyable fruits of freedom itself. Once the hard egalitarian goals of the ERA were unmasked, the constitutional amendment was doomed to fail. And the one who unmasked them was the formidable Mrs. Schlafly, maternal feminist par excellence.

WOMEN UNDER FREEDOM

Back before the fight over the ERA, before even the equalizing legislation and court rulings of the second wave, all the way back in the 1940s, a conservative feminist made a prediction about what would happen under conditions of freedom and opportunity for women. Popular playwright and member of Congress Clare Boothe Luce wrote:

> It is time to leave the question of the role of women in society up to Mother Nature—a difficult lady to fool. You have only to give women the same opportunities as men, and you will soon find out what is or is not in their nature. What is in women's nature to do they will do, and you won't be able to stop them. But you will also find, and so will they, that what is not in their nature, even if they are given every opportunity, they will not do, and you won't be able to make them do it.[91]

In Luce's day, sex-role stereotypes still powerfully limited women's choices. More than half a century later, women enjoy the equality of opportunity of which she spoke. We have, in effect, run the experiment and can observe the results. By examining what women have and haven't chosen to do, we can begin to discern who was closer to Mother Nature—Mary Wollstonecraft insisting that the sexes, once freed, would make the same choices, or Hannah

More suggesting that women would always prevail in the domestic sphere and express themselves as the caregivers of the species.

By the 1980s and 1990s, American women were entering the workplace in record numbers, filling the colleges, law schools, and medical schools, starting businesses, joining sports teams, and enjoying and contending with opportunities beyond those of any women in history. They were venturing in droves far beyond the domestic sphere.

Yet gender roles persisted. Majorities of working mothers (62 percent) still "say they would prefer to work part time," according to a 2009 Pew Research Center survey, which also found that "an overwhelming majority [of working fathers] (79 percent) say they prefer full-time work.[92] Only one in five say they would choose part-time work." Phyllis Schlafly's claim that "most women want to be a wife, mother and homemaker and are happy in that role" carried more than a grain of truth. No matter how many times they were denied, the insights of Hannah More and Frances Willard have remained salient: there are specifically feminine graces and virtues and a specifically female penchant for tenderness, care, and nurture.

These realities are reflected not only in women's preference for part-time work but also in their predominance in the caring professions.

Even today, at a time when hardline egalitarian feminism is dominant in education, the media, and the women's movement, women continue to far outnumber men in fields like nursing, social work, pediatrics, veterinary medicine, and early childhood education. Meanwhile, men? To them, "the world [is] essentially a theater for heroism," in the words of the great nineteenth-century psychologist William James.[93] They continue to far outnumber women in the saving and rescuing vocations of policeman, firefighter, and soldier.

Even as barriers have come down for the minorities of women who do want to join the Marines or play football—and social scientists confirm that nearly one-fifth of women defy the stereotypes of their sex—men and women by and large gravitate to different sex roles.[94] The egalitarian dream of an androgynous, gender-integrated society, still celebrated in books such as Sheryl Sandberg's *Lean In*, has shown no sign of materializing.

In a 2008 study in the *Journal of Personality and Social Psychology*, a group of international researchers compared data on gender and personality across fifty-five nations.[95] In all the countries studied, women tended to be more cooperative, nurturing, risk averse, and emotionally expressive; men were more competitive, reckless, and emotionally flat. Here is what I find most fascinating: personality differences between men and women are the largest and most robust in prosperous, egalitarian, post-industrial societies. According to the authors, "Higher levels of human development—including long and healthy life, equal access to knowledge and education, and economic wealth—were the main nation-level predictors of sex difference variation across cultures." A *New York Times* story summarized the study this way: "It looks as if personality differences between men and women are smaller in traditional cultures like India's or Zimbabwe's than in the Netherlands or the United States. A husband and a stay-at-home wife in a patriarchal Botswanan clan seem to be more alike than a working couple in Denmark or France. The more Venus and Mars have equal rights and similar jobs, the more their personalities seem to diverge."[96]

Why should this be the case? The authors hypothesize that prosperous, egalitarian nations offer more opportunities for self-actualization. Wealth, freedom, and education empower men and women to be who they are. We have seen that gay liberation is more likely to emerge in advanced, post-industrial societies; it looks as though such societies afford heterosexuals, too, more opportunities to embrace their gender identities. This cross-cultural research is far from conclusive, but it is intriguing and has great explanatory power. Just think: what if gender difference turns out to be a phenomenon not of oppression but rather of social well-being?

The grand experiment of the last half-century confirms, then, the paradox of egalitarian feminism: when women are liberated from the domestic sphere, granted their full Enlightenment freedoms to pursue happiness, and no longer sequestered in the role of nurturer, many, perhaps most, persist in giving priority to the domestic sphere.

Most Americans, ever practical, seem unbothered by this outcome. They have implicitly adopted the eclectic approach I call freedom feminism, which insists on legal equality and opposes efforts to impose stereotypical roles, but recognizes that men and women will typically employ their freedom in distinctive ways—and will find the basic conventions of femininity and masculinity to be natural, attractive, and powerful sources of meaning and happiness. Freedom feminists appreciate that efforts to obliterate gender roles can be just as intolerant as efforts to enforce them. For them, persistent differences between the sexes, under conditions of freedom, can be a sign of social well-being. Freedom feminism is at peace, not at war, with abiding human aspiration.

The same cannot be said of egalitarian feminism. Although they seldom mention it in public, egalitarian feminists are often profoundly disappointed with what they see as contemporary women's false and self-defeating choices. Unable to accept the evidence of experience, they are driven to develop theories of subtle coercion and deep institutional injustice still operating to oppress women. And it is these feminist theorists who have captured the organized women's movement.

Activists may have lost the battle over the ERA, but in the wake of that defeat they won the political infrastructure of feminism. Historian Sara Evans cites the words of an ERA leader on lessons learned from that epic battle: "The struggle over [the amendment's] ratification has provided the greatest political training ground for women in the history of the world."[97] As Evans notes, after 1982, the momentum shifted and "feminists of all persuasions began to face the necessity to dig in for the long haul."

Once dug in, few ERA refugees bothered to reengage with maternal feminists or to address the actual, practical issues of post-liberation womanhood. Instead, mortified and angered by their loss, many retreated into advocacy groups, research centers, and feminist theory enclaves in the universities, where they used their considerable skills to pursue their agenda by other means.

In their academic isolation, they expanded their analysis of the patriarchy that they insist holds millions of American women in its thrall, unconscious of their servitude. Persuaded of the reality of female victimhood, they saw no point in engaging with unbelievers. They rarely consulted their academic colleagues down the hall in, say, the economics or statistics department. Most male academics maintained a judicious silence, and few female scholars were inclined to challenge sisters who had made women's issues their specialty. As a result, today, in women's research centers across the nation, the hardliners rule unopposed.

3

CONTEMPORARY FEMINISM AND A WAY FORWARD

FEMINIST THEORY AND ITS DISCONTENTS

In the summer of 1985, Virginia Held, a professor at the City University of New York, announced in a premier philosophy journal that feminist theorists had initiated an intellectual revolution comparable to those of "Copernicus, Darwin, and Freud."[98] Indeed, said Held, "some feminists think the latest revolution will be even more profound." What they had discovered was the "sex/gender system"—a pervasive system by which men oppress women. "Now that the sex/gender system has become visible to us," said Held, "we can see it everywhere."[99]

Held and her sister theorists believed that every human achievement bears the impress of patriarchy: literature, philosophy, science, music, language. It is not enough to reform a few laws or change a few traditions or customs. You cannot simply "add women and stir." The system itself must be dismantled. The theory drew inspiration from the egalitarian writings of Wollstonecraft, Mill, and Stanton. But it also grew out of the radical politics of the 1960s and is informed by the philosophy of Karl Marx and his heirs, such as Herbert Marcuse, Frantz Fanon, and Michel Foucault. Stirring feminism into this tradition generated such Copernican discoveries as this one from legal theorist Catharine MacKinnon: "I think that sexual desire in women, at least in this culture, is socially constructed as that by which we come to want our own self-annihilation."[100]

There are serious scholars in women's studies. UC Davis anthropologist Sarah Blaffer Hrdy, Brandeis sociologist Janet Zollinger Giele, UCLA literary scholar Anne Mellor, and Hunter College classicist Sarah Pomeroy—to name only a few—are models of academic excellence. Most departments include a share of solid, non-ideological scholars who offer straightforward courses in women's history or women and literature. But in too many colleges and universities, ideologically inflamed, statistically challenged "theorists" set the tone and the agenda.[101]

Students who enroll in typical introductory women's studies courses are not likely to learn about the conservative roots of women's emancipation. Even the egalitarian thinkers of the first wave are sometimes given short shrift. Textbooks in feminist theory often present Mary Wollstonecraft, Elizabeth Cady Stanton, and Susan B. Anthony under the rubric of "liberal feminism." Liberal feminism is then described as a relic of the past, limited to the needs of middle-class women in capitalist societies, long since surpassed by more inclusive theories. These include "gynocentric" feminism, which views women as different—and far better—than men, and assorted versions of Marxist, socialist, radical, multiracial, and post-colonial feminisms. Here is a typical passage from *Thinking about Women*, a popular introductory text:

> Because liberal feminism is based on the concept of equal access to social institutions, it does not provide a criticism of the very structure of those institutions as a source of women's oppression. . . . In distinct contrast to this perspective, socialist and radical feminists argue that the success of liberal feminism only puts some women on a par with men without transforming the conditions of oppression that produce gender as well as class and race inequality. Thus, socialist and radical feminists have more thoroughly criticized the structure of Western, capitalist, patriarchal social institutions.[102]

Bell hooks' *Feminist Theory: From Margin to Center* makes the same point as the textbook, only more acerbically: "Bourgeois class biases have led many feminist theorists to develop ideas that have little or no relation to the lived experiences of most women, theories that are not useful for making feminist revolution."[103] She singles out "liberal individualism" as a primary impediment to the revolution she has in mind.[104] For her, former Supreme Court Justice Sandra Day O'Connor is a living example of the failure of liberal feminism: "Women like O'Connor . . . will exercise power alongside men even as they continue to support white supremacy, capitalism and patriarchy."[105]

Such arguments will be familiar to anyone immersed in contemporary feminist theory. But they do not stand up to scrutiny. Let's start with the idea that "liberal feminism" is classist, racist, and tailored to the needs and aspirations of white bourgeois women. It is certainly true that the early feminists, including Elizabeth Cady Stanton, Susan B. Anthony, and Frances Willard, were sometimes insensitive to race and class injustice. Like all iconic moral leaders, they had feet of clay. Through selective quotation, they can appear to be narrow-minded and reactionary. Stanton and Anthony opposed the Fifteenth Amendment on the grounds that it granted the vote to "ignorant" black and immigrant males—while excluding educated, native-born women like themselves. Even the saintly Frances Willard sometimes equivocated on racial issues.[106] But the personal failings of these leaders should not distract us from the justice of their cause. The feminist foremothers of the first wave, despite their personal limitations, were promoting *universal* human ideals. The rights to vote, to be educated, to enter a marriage of equals, to flourish—these are not the special province of white women, middle-class women, American women, or Western women. They are rights that belong to human beings everywhere. And everywhere, both women and men are claiming them.

Today, in countries like Burma, Iran, Cambodia, Saudi Arabia, and Egypt, courageous women are fighting for the identical rights pioneered by their Western "liberal feminist" foremothers. Consider Zin Mar Aung, a thirty-six-year-old activist from Burma. Aung, whom I heard speak at a 2011 international women's rights conference, spent eleven years in solitary confinement in a Burmese jail for the crime of carrying pro-democracy flyers and expressing solidarity with Nobel laureate Aung San Suu Kyi. She told us she survived her confinement by reciting a poem over and over again: "Someone can imprison your body, but not your mind." What did she do once she was freed from prison? She immediately began protesting again. "We try to deliver the message: Democracy is not only for the West, but for all human beings."[107] The same is true for the ideals promoted by More, Wollstonecraft, Willard, Stanton, and Anthony.

What about the idea that feminism is authentic only when it is revolutionary? This claim both denigrates the vast achievements of more moderate traditions of reform and disregards the dangers inherent in radical social transformation. Feminist theory texts sometimes go to great lengths to warn about the limits and hazards of moderate liberal feminism—but I have yet to find one that warns of the dangers of radical social engineering.[108] "Feminist revolution" is celebrated without any indication that utopian ventures—from the American communes of the nineteenth century to the catastrophic Marxist governments of the twentieth century—have often produced immense human misery.

This book will not pause to dissect the Marxist, socialist, radical, multiracial, or post-colonial schools of feminism. Too often these are vehicles for repressive ideologies that have proved hostile to the needs of most women. And there is not a scintilla of evidence that women, outside of the narrowest intellectual circles, take them seriously. If they were put to a vote, the women of the world would surely reject them. Women of all races, ethnic groups, social classes, and gender identities aspire to freedom, opportunity, and self-determination, and they are fully capable of distinguishing progress from revolution.

Freedom feminists, unlike their radical sisters, do not see patriarchal domination "everywhere." Certainly not in the United States. What we see is a nation that has realized the aspirations of our feminist foremothers. Women's equality is a great American success story. The hardline theorists see no story of success. Pick up a feminist theory textbook, and you are likely to find elaborate conspiracy theories about "male hegemony." American college women are among the freest, most fortunate people in the world. But in many feminist classrooms they are taught that they inhabit an oppressive society where women are conditioned to subordination.

In their eye-opening book *Professing Feminism: Education and Indoctrination in Women's Studies*, two once-committed feminist professors, Daphne Patai and Noretta Koertge, describe the "sea of propaganda" that overwhelms the contemporary feminist classroom.[109] They show how idealistic female students are changed into "relentless grievance collectors."[110] The historian Christine Rosen, in her 2002 report on the five leading women's studies textbooks, found them all to be hostile to traditional marriage, stay-at-home mothers, and the culture of romance. They were also rife with falsehoods, half-truths, and "deliberately misleading sisterly sophistries."[111]

FEMINIST MS.INFORMATION

Over the years, I have looked carefully at feminist theory claims about women and violence, depression, eating disorders, pay equity, and education. What

I have found is that most—not all, but most—of the victim statistics are misleading, confused, or deliberately inaccurate. Consider the highly praised *Penguin Atlas of Women in the World* (2009), by academic feminist Joni Seager, chair of the Hunter College geography department.[112] The atlas was named "reference book of the year" by the American Library Association when it was first published and is now in its fourth edition. "Nobody should be without this book," urged feminist icon Gloria Steinem.[113] "A wealth of fascinating information," said *The Washington Post*.[114] Fascinating, it may be. But the information is skewed and, at least in one instance, flat-out false.

One color-coded map illustrates how women are kept "in their place" by restrictions on their mobility, dress, and behavior. On this score, the United States is ranked with Somalia, Uganda, Yemen, Niger, and Libya. All are coded with the same shade of green to indicate places where "patriarchal assumptions" operate in "potent combination with fundamentalist religious interpretations."[115] Seager's logic? She notes that in parts of Uganda, a man can claim an unmarried woman as his wife by raping her. The United States gets the same rating because "State legislators enacted 301 anti-abortion measures between 1995 and 2001."[116] Never mind that the Ugandan practice is barbaric, that U.S. abortion law is exceptionally liberal among the nations of the world, and that the political activism and controversy surrounding abortion in the United States is a sign of a free democracy working out its disagreements in a way inconceivable in Uganda.

On another map, the United States gets the same rating for domestic violence as Uganda and Haiti. Seager supports this claim by citing a ubiquitous emergency-room fiction: "22–35 percent of women who visit a hospital emergency room do so because of domestic violence."[117] This false statistic has been refuted many times, but it still appears in feminist textbooks.[118] The actual figure is less than 1 percent, documented in studies by the Centers for Disease Control and the Justice Department's Bureau of Justice Statistics.[119] Surely victims of domestic abuse are best served by truth and high-quality research. They do not need gender politics and exaggeration— even if well-intentioned.

Reasonable people can always debate statistical findings, but feminist textbooks do not seem interested in debate. Most ignore studies that show low rates of victimization or injustice, no matter how rigorous and fair-minded they may be, and embrace as gospel those that show high levels, no matter how dubious and slanted they may be. Of course, the literature on feminism is vast and complex; there are bound to be some mistakes. What I and other critics have found are not "some mistakes." What we have found is a large body of false information that appears to be immune to correction.[120] Consider how most feminist professors, let alone activists, discuss the infamous gender wage gap.

In her examination of women's studies textbooks, Christine Rosen found that all of them uncritically repeat the claim that the wage gap between men and women in the United States is caused by workplace discrimination. But the 23-cent gap is simply the difference between the average earnings of all men and women working full-time. It does not account for differences in occupations, positions, education, job tenure, or actual hours worked. ("Full time" can mean anything more than 35 hours per week—leaving a large range for variation.) When economists consider the wage gap, they find that pay disparities are almost entirely the result of women's different life preferences—what they choose to study in school, where they work, and how they balance their home and career. A thorough 2009 study by the U.S. Department of Labor examined more than fifty peer-reviewed papers on the subject and concluded that the wage gap "may be almost entirely the result of individual choices being made by both male and female workers."[121] In addition to differences in education and training, the review found that women are more likely than men to leave the workforce to take care of children or older parents. There were so many differences in pay-related choices that the researchers were unable to specify even a residual effect that might be the result of discrimination.

Wage-gap activists at the American Association of University Women and the National Women's Law Center say that even when we control for relevant variables, women still earn less. But it always turns out that they have omitted one or two crucial variables. Why play this game? Why teach it to students? Consider the case of pharmacists. Almost half of all pharmacists are female, yet as a group, women earn only 85 percent of what their male counterparts earn. Why should that be? After all, male and female pharmacists are doing the same job with roughly identical educations. There must be some hidden discrimination at play. But according to the 2009 National Pharmacist Workforce Survey, male pharmacists work on average 2.4 hours more per week, have more job experience, and more of them own their own stores.[122] A 2012 *New York Times* article tells a similar story about women in medicine: "Female doctors are more likely to be pediatricians than higher-paid cardiologists. They are more likely to work part time. And even those working full time put in 7 percent fewer hours a week than men. They are also much more likely to take extended leaves, most often to give birth and start a family."[123]

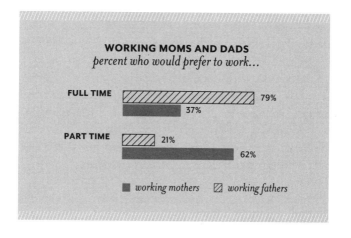

WORKING MOMS AND DADS
percent who would prefer to work...

FULL TIME — working fathers 79%, working mothers 37%

PART TIME — working fathers 21%, working mothers 62%

■ *working mothers* ▨ *working fathers*

There are exceptions, but most workplace pay gaps and glass ceilings vanish when one accounts for these factors. No doubt there are still unscrupulous employers out there who will try to pay Jill 73 cents and Jack one dollar for the same job. Thanks to conservatives and liberals of the early second wave we have laws against that. But evidence of systemic gender wage discrimination by American employers is nowhere to be found.

Women's groups do occasionally acknowledge that the pay gap is explained by women's life choices, as the AAUW does in its 2007 *Behind the Pay Gap*.[124] But this admission is qualified: they insist that women's choices are not truly free. Women who decide, say, to stay home with children or to become pediatricians rather than cardiologists are driven by sexist stereotypes. "Women's personal choices are. . . . fraught with inequities," says the AAUW.[125] It speaks of women being "pigeonholed" into "pink-collar" jobs in health and education. According to the National Organization for Women, powerful sexist stereotypes "steer" women and men "toward different education, training, and career paths" and family roles.[126]

But is it really sexist stereotypes and social conditioning that best explain women's vocational preferences and their special attachment to children? Aren't most American women free and self-determining human beings? The women's groups need to show—not dogmatically assert—that women's choices are not free. And they need to explain why, by contrast, the life choices they promote are the authentic ones—what women truly want and what will make them happier and more fulfilled.

Still, it remains true that women are economically more vulnerable than men, and it is mainly women with children who fill the poverty rolls. Even if employers are not to blame, we cannot just throw up our hands and say there is nothing to be done. Liberals will favor European-style government programs that help alleviate poverty and make it easier for mothers to combine the demands of home and work. Conservatives will question the effectiveness of "big government" programs and will look for ways to address what they see as the root cause of female poverty: out-of-wedlock births and missing fathers. But in most academic feminist programs, the conservative point of view is never given a respectful hearing.

The prevalence of propaganda and one-sidedness is not without consequence. As a regular campus lecturer, I routinely encounter gender studies majors who have drunk deeply of the feminist Kool-Aid. They are generally intelligent, sensitive, socially concerned young women. But they have come to regard the grim radical feminist worldview as incontrovertible truth. Some of them seem to regard alternative opinions as a form of hate speech. Most are simply astonished and confused that reasoned, empirically based arguments contrary to their classroom teachings could even exist. This is the opposite of what a college education should be. It is also a barrier to the emergence of a capacious, open feminism that seeks to engage the real opportunities and problems of contemporary womanhood.

There is a second such barrier, in the world of politics and the media.

THE FEMINIST BRAIN TRUST

The National Council for Research on Women (NCRW), launched in 1981, is a network of 120 women's research and policy centers. It includes mainstream organizations such as Catalyst, Hadassah, and the YWCA, but two-thirds of its members are academic centers at schools such as Harvard, Wellesley, Stanford, and Rutgers. Finally, members include several activist research institutes like the American Association for University Women, the Institute for Women's Policy Research, the Ms. Foundation, and the National Women's Law Center. Together these groups constitute what might be called the feminist brain trust. Their research provides answers to fundamental questions: How do women live, work, and learn? What do they value? What laws are needed? "Research powers a revolution," says an NCRW promotional video.[127] But what if the research is unreliable? And who is asking for a revolution?

In December 2011, I took part in an Oxford Union–style debate on the website of *The Economist*. The motion before the house: "a woman's place is at work." Arguing for the motion was Linda Basch, president of the NCRW. Her condemnation of domesticity was less harsh than Betty Friedan's or that of the women's studies textbooks, but it was just as censorious. Right out of the gate she said: "Women belong in the workplace. It is right for families, communities, the economy, and, most importantly, for women so that they can live to their full potential as productive and self-reliant individuals."[128]

Basch's insistence that women have only one place, the workplace, surprised many readers and even the debate's moderator. It did not surprise me, because I was familiar with NCRW. Many of its most influential members remain captivated by 1970s-style egalitarian feminism. They remain true to the ERA dream of a gender-integrated society where sex roles have vanished. Why, ask the NCRW feminists, should there be so many more men in math and engineering than women? What explains the over-representation of men on Sunday morning news programs? Why do so few women hold public office? And, most urgently, why do so many women contribute to their own second-class status by giving priority to home and family over career? These are good questions, and there are no easy answers. But NCRW groups have a ready answer: women are being held back by unconscious bias, hostile climates, and internalized oppression. Other, more innocent explanations—such as the possibility that women and men, taken as groups, differ in some respects—are ruled out of bounds. The NCRW egalitarians have their own research that they think shows the presence of ubiquitous, albeit invisible, discrimination, and they have hundreds of activist initiatives to set things right.

Because it successfully claims to represent women, the NCRW attracts such heavyweight donors as Pfizer, Goldman Sachs, GE, Time Warner, Toyota, Morgan Stanley, Bloomberg, and American Express. Forty-three college presidents and chancellors have joined the organization's "President's Circle."[129] When journalists, policymakers, and legislators address topics such as the wage gap, gender and education, or women's health, they turn to one of the NCRW's two thousand experts for enlightenment. So the network flourishes and grows.

In 2006, the NCRW published a major report entitled *Gains and Gaps: A Look at the World's Women*. There is much to admire in this report. It includes crucial findings on honor killings in Pakistan, acid burnings in Bangladesh, and genital mutilation in Mali. But its authors depict American women as part of a worldwide system of oppression. While it concedes that women in developing countries face a "relatively more dire situation," it insists that American women are "far from standing above the problems faced by women around the world." As the authors explain, "Deeply ingrained gendering occurs in all societies," and the United States is no exception. "US women continue to confront inequalities in the workforce, increasing attacks on reproductive rights, and constraints on their ascendance to leadership positions . . . particularly in the political arena."[130]

But is it necessarily discrimination, constraints, inequality, and "attacks" that explain where women are today in the United States? Or might it instead be that, in following the feminist dream of "not being at the mercy of the world, but as builder and designer," women do things their own way? NCRW officials have a special word for this kind of inquiry: "push-back."[131] The American Association of University Women (AAUW), one of the NCRW's more influential member organizations, refers to skeptics and dissidents as "adversaries" and has put them on notice.

> Our adversaries know that AAUW is a force to be reckoned with . . . We are issuing fair warning—we are breaking through barriers. We mean it; we've done it before; and we are "coming after them" again . . . and again and again, if we have to! All of us, all the time.[132]

To appreciate the damage wrought by the NCRW lobby, one has only to look at its influence in the United States Congress. Consider, for example, the misleadingly labeled Paycheck Fairness Act. The bill was based on the premise that the 1963 Equal Pay Act, which bans sex discrimination in the workplace, had failed; for proof, proponents pointed out that for every dollar men earn, women earn just 77 cents. The legislation would make employers liable not only for intentional sex discrimination (something they have long been liable for) but also for "lingering effects of past discrimination." What does that mean? Employers had no idea. Universities, for example, pay professors in the business school more than those in the school of social work. They point to market forces as the justification. But according to the gender theory that informed the Paycheck Fairness Act, market forces are tainted by past discrimination. The act noted helpfully that "pay disparities" resulting from "lingering effects of past discrimination" have been "spread and perpetuated through commerce."[133] And it went on to provide for expeditious class-action lawsuits with punitive damages for violation of its vague, open-ended standards.

Groups like the U.S. Chamber of Commerce—some of whose members are NCRW donors!—protested that the law could be "devastating" to American business.[134] Even the *Washington Post* and the *Boston Globe* urged Congress to reject it and dismissed it as "flawed."[135] The *Globe* wisely asked, "What if a company offers a higher salary for retail workers in a more dangerous location, and more men sign up?

What if a male worker leverages a job offer into a higher salary? Should these be illegal acts?" After several votes in the House and Senate, the Paycheck Fairness Act went down to defeat in June 2012. One of the bill's sponsors, Senator Barbara Mikulski (D-MD), vowed she and her allies would return to fight another day: "I'm putting my lipstick back on and I am combat ready to keep on fighting."[136] Why invest so much time, money, and lipstick for such an unreasonable end?

The Paycheck Fairness Act and other ill-advised legislative proposals (such as the "Fulfilling the Potential of Women in Academic Science and Engineering Act," which would subject those fields to feminist training programs) were built on years of tendentious advocacy research. Like much of the NCRW agenda, such laws would set women against men, empower trial lawyers and activists, perpetuate falsehoods about the status of women, and create havoc in a fragile economy. Were there a conservative or moderate wing inside the women's education network, the errors and half-truths in the scholarship would have been challenged and corrected long ago, and better legislation proposed. No such wing exists.

Powerful NCRW member groups like the National Women's Law Center, the Institute for Women's Policy Research, and the AAUW see the world as a battlefront in a zero-sum struggle between men and women. Their job is to side with the women. Few women see life as a Manichean struggle between Venus and Mars; the activist NCRW groups represent a vanishingly small constituency. But, for the moment, those groups set the agenda.

The most serious damage wrought by the women's brain trust is not legislative but cultural. It has shaped the worldview of millions of educated professional women. Consider, for example, the "Women in the World Summit" held in March 2012.[137] For three days, more than two thousand professional women gathered at Lincoln Center in New York City for a glittering conference on international women's rights. With generous funding from HP, Bank of America, Toyota, Intel, Coca-Cola, and other corporations, the entire event was exquisitely choreographed. The program was filled with celebrities such as Angelina Jolie, Meryl Streep, and Oprah and star journalists such as Barbara Walters, Christiane Amanpour, and Andrea Mitchell.

Organized by Tina Brown, editor of *The Daily Beast* and *Newsweek*, the summit was supposed to recognize and assist those who are working to advance the status of women—often lowly and precarious—in the developing world. And it did indeed feature a succession of impressive women's rights activists (including several men) from across the globe. On one panel after another, the audience heard from change agents successfully combating child marriage in Pakistan, femicide in the Congo, and genital cutting in Senegal.

But when American women took the stage, the Summit morphed into a feminist grievance-fest. The Americans—famous, accomplished, powerful, and wealthy—seemed to think that the freedom-fighters from the developing world were important mainly as an inspiration to American women in their own equally urgent struggle against oppression. An impassioned Democratic leader, Nancy Pelosi, declared that, "whatever the arena is, it is stacked against us." Her interviewer, journalist Pat Mitchell, concurred and described the current environment in the United States as a "nightmare." Jane Harman—former Democratic congresswoman, now president of the Woodrow Wilson Center—quipped that there is no glass ceiling keeping women down, "just a thick layer of men" (this so delighted the audience that she repeated it the next day). Former Secretary of State Madeleine Albright, when asked why there are still so few women in power in the United States, exclaimed, "Men!" Albright continued, "People say, there are not enough 'qualified' women. That is one of the biggest bullshit things I have ever heard. There are men who do not want to see women in power." She concluded, "There is a special place in Hell for women who don't help each other." But her presentation was more about vilifying men than helping women.

The highlight of the summit was an appearance by Secretary of State Hillary Clinton. Secretary Clinton re-focused attention on the heroism of women dissidents in places like Pakistan, Burma, and Egypt. But then came the pivot:

> Why extremists always focus on women remains a mystery to me. But they all seem to. It doesn't matter what country they're in or what religion they claim. They all want to control women. They want to control how we dress. They want to control how we act. They even want to control the decisions we make about our own health and our own bodies. . . . Yes, it is hard to believe, but even here at home, we have to stand up for women's rights and reject efforts to marginalize any one of us, because America needs to set an example for the entire world.

She proceeded to compare the alleged bravery of Sandra Fluke (the Georgetown University law student then in the news for demanding that the university's health insurance cover birth control) to that of Burmese dissidents—praising women who are "assuming the risks that come with sticking your neck out, whether you are a democracy activist in Burma or a Georgetown law student in the United States." The audience was overjoyed. But the awkwardness of Clinton's comparison was dramatized by the presence of Zin Mar Aung, the thirty-six-year-old Burmese activist who spent eleven years in solitary confinement for the crime of carrying pro-democracy flyers.

At the time of the summit, Americans were contentiously debating whether or not Catholic (and other) institutions should be required to pay for their employees' and students' birth control pills, and what if any procedures women might be required to go through before obtaining an abortion. Americans are deeply divided on the ethics of abortion. Among women, according to a 2011 Gallup poll, 50 percent are generally pro-choice, 44 percent are generally pro-life, and only 29 percent want abortion to be legal "in any circumstance" (the breakdown for men was only slightly different).[138] The impassioned argument over the issue is not a "war on women." It is called democracy. Burmese activists such as Zin Mar Aung are risking their lives, and suffering grievously, to win this form of government for themselves. For American women on one side of our democratic debates to compare their circumstances to those of the Burmese freedom fighters was insulting and embarrassing.

The Women in the World Summit juxtaposed brave, calm, fiercely determined women and men who are struggling against female subjugation in some of the most benighted parts of the world with a spectacle of American self-absorption. It illustrated how feminist shibboleths can be offered, and accepted, by people who would never speak so loosely, or listen so uncritically, in other domains. Women such as Jane Harman and Hillary Clinton are justly respected for their intellects and accomplishments. They are accustomed to thinking critically and speaking carefully. Yet the moment they address current American "women's issues" they sound as if they had been brainwashed by a feminist theory textbook. And thousands of successful professional women cheer them on. How did this come to be?

Secretary Clinton and other summit luminaries are not hardline feminists. Nor are most of the members of Congress who support reckless feminist legislation. But they listen to the NCRW groups and take their research seriously. The AAUW, the National Women's Law Center, and hundreds of women's studies departments across the country promulgate the recognized "women's positions" on questions of policy and culture. Too often, what we know about women we learn from them. But they cannot be trusted.

Feminism has devolved into a one-party system. But a flourishing women's movement needs both conservative and liberal wings. From the dawn of feminism until very recently, moderate and conservative women have corrected the excesses of their more radical sisters and kept the movement anchored in practical reality and mainstream sensibilities. In this light, today's feminist antics—the sorry state of campus women's studies, the harmful legislative agenda promoted by the intellectually suspect NCRW groups, the comportment of otherwise reasonable women at the Women in the World Summit—should be seen not as the end of feminism but as cries for help. Fortunately, a rescue party is at hand. Its name is freedom feminism.

CONCLUSION

THE FREEDOM FEMINIST AGENDA

The historical women's movement, at its best and most effective, was representative, broad-based, and purposive. Seeking to improve society rather than turn it upside-down, the movement won many famous victories and earned the gratitude and respect of posterity. Today's movement has harnessed the prestige of historic feminism, but its aims and methods are those of a narrow, intellectually corrupt, special-interest group. It does not have to be this way. What follows are five suggestions for a revival of the freedom feminist movement.

1. TAKE BACK REASON

There is an urgent need to correct more than forty years of feminist advocacy research. At the present time, a study produced by an NCRW organization or similar group must be presumed to be manipulated in the service of gender ideology. That is a shame: women who study and write about women's issues should not be expected to check their critical facilities at the door. Sound policies on problems such as violence against women, gender and education, and workplace equity must be predicated on sound research. Legislators, educators, and the public are getting too little trustworthy information on women's issues, and political discourse and policy are suffering as a result.

Fortunately, there is a growing body of serious empirical research on these issues, much of it by women. Diana Furchtgott-Roth, former chief economist in the U.S. Department of Labor, has written a trenchant analysis on the wage gap, the glass ceiling, and the feminization of poverty in *Women's Figures: An Illustrated Guide to the Economic Progress of Women*.[139] Cornell's Stephen Ceci and Wendy Williams have done meticulous research on the dearth of women in the physical sciences and engineering that makes hash of many of the claims of women-in-science political activists.[140] Several economists have produced exemplary studies on the wage gap, the effects of quotas on corporate boards, and why men and women differ in career choices.[141] One even finds occasional useful research at NCRW affiliates. In 2012, the Women and Politics Institute published an excellent study on women in politics that someone should show to Madeleine Albright.[142]

This research displays an increasing self-confidence and willingness to challenge the dogmas of the feminist brain trust. Women of the freedom feminism wing need to give solid research greater prominence and call out political figures and journalists who rely on dubious data and pretend that no alternative exists. Most of all, this wing needs to assume a leading role in drafting a new platform of policies and cultural standards concerned with the real issues confronting modern women.

2. BE PRO-WOMEN BUT NOT MALE-AVERSE

The current women's lobby thinks of men as a rival camp. Not only are men denigrated, but their problems are ignored or explained away. There is, for example, an alarming and growing gender gap in education that shows male students falling far behind female students. We now have thousands of programs to strengthen girls academically but almost nothing for boys. A reformed women's movement would acknowledge that the health, education, and welfare of males are pressing public issues. Men and women complement each other. We are not on separate teams competing for one trophy. This is not a zero-sum competition; we are not natural adversaries. We are dancing partners like Fred Astaire and Ginger Rogers. Our fates are inextricably tied—if one is in trouble, so is the other.

3. PURSUE HAPPINESS

Consider the Netherlands. Dutch women are among the freest, best-educated, and happiest women on the planet. In studies of life satisfaction and well-being, Dutch women (and men too) consistently score at the top. More than 70 percent of Dutch working women work part time—but when asked if they would like to work more, the vast majority say no.

Is it because they are held back by inadequate child-care policies? No, even childless women and those with grown children abjure full-time employment. "It has to do with personal freedom," says Ellen de Bruin, a Dutch psychologist and the author of *Dutch Women Don't Get Depressed*. "What is important," she says, is that "women in the Netherlands are free to choose whatever they want to do."[143]

But the Netherlands would get failing grades for workplace equity from the U.S. women's lobby. A United Nations gender equity committee recently censured the Netherlands for the "low number of women who are economically independent."[144] A 2010 *Slate* article is less censorious: "Women in the Netherlands work less, have lesser titles, and a big gender gap, and they love it."[145] The author concludes by advising her American sisters, "Maybe we'd be better-off if we could relax and go Dutch."[146] That will not be the answer for all women, but why should it not be an option respected by all?

4. RESPECT FEMALE DIVERSITY

Twenty-first century feminism must learn to accept women as they are, not as they were supposed to be according to egalitarian specifications drawn up in 1978. Women are various. Some are as dedicated to careers as men, but many are not. Despite nearly 40 years of gender-neutral pronouns and harsh denunciations of women's traditional roles, domestic life remains a vital priority for millions. And no amount of consciousness raising or cajoling has discouraged women from pursuing pink-collar jobs in the helping and caring professions. Among New York's celebrated vocational schools, Fashion Industry High is 98 percent female; Automotive High is 3 percent female. Freedom feminism welcomes and respects the choices of both groups of young women. The British comedic writer Caitlin Moran calls herself a "strident feminist"; but many passages in her funny new book *How to Be a Woman* capture the spirit of freedom feminism. What is feminism? she asks. "Simply the belief that women should be as free as men, however nuts, dim, deluded, badly dressed, fat, receding, lazy, and smug they might be."[147] Says Moran:

> You can be whatever you want, so long as you're sure it's what you actually want, rather than one of two equally dodgy choices foisted on you. Because the purpose of feminism isn't to make a particular type of woman. The idea that there are inherently wrong and inherently right "types" of women is what's screwed feminism for so long—this belief that "we" wouldn't accept slaggy birds, dim birds, birds that bitch, birds that have

cleaners, birds that stay home with their kids, birds that drive Pink Mini Metros with POWERED BY FAIRY DUST! bumper stickers. . . . You know what? Feminism will have all of you.[148]

5. NO POLITICAL LITMUS TESTS

Freedom feminists can be liberal, conservative, or libertarian. They can differ over abortion, the wage gap, and the role of government in the lives of women. They can strike different balances between family and career. In the spirit of pluralism and democratic coalition-building, they can even work together for concrete ends, while standing on different philosophical bedrock. What they must share is respect for considered differences of opinion and choice, insistence that debate and scholarship be reasoned and evidence-based, commitment to improving the lives of women, recognition that the sexes are equal but different, and devotion to Enlightenment democratic principles.

To the extent that the hardliners share these commitments, they can still play a critical role. Consider Eve Ensler again. Her twisted lectures such as the one at Harvard, and the violent portrayal of heterosexuality in her famous play, *The Vagina Monologues*, have alienated many. But her work in the developing world is a different story. Over the years, she has been personally active in promoting women's rights in forbidding places such as Rwanda, Haiti, and Afghanistan. In recent years, she has been working in the Democratic Republic of the Congo, where thousands of women have been brutally raped and tortured by gangs of soldiers. One frustrated former United Nations official was dismayed by the "appalling and grotesque indifference by the world community" to the fate of the Congolese women. But Ensler is not indifferent. She is waging a campaign to raise world awareness and bring support to these women. Ensler's perspective on the United States and American women may be bizarre, but her efforts in the Congo are nothing short of heroic.

Or consider the international women's groups such as the Feminist Majority, the Women in the World Foundation, and Equality Now. These groups are aggressively targeting human rights violations such as the sex trafficking of women and children in India, female genital mutilation in Mali, and lashings of women in Iran. This is admirable and necessary work that both conservative and liberal women can endorse and support. The two groups will never agree on the Paycheck Fairness Act or whether the paucity of female electrical engineers is due to sexist conspiracy. But there could be a powerful and effective consensus on the need to help millions of women around the world who are struggling against honor killings, genital cutting, acid attacks, forced marriages, and lashings.

There are grassroots women's groups everywhere in the developing world who are engaged in reforming societies. Imagine the power of an American women's movement that did not exclude conservative and religious women. What if the modern heirs to Hannah More and Frances Willard were part of an ecumenical coalition? Today's feminist movement is a hostile environment for faith-based, family-centered, conservative women. Yet just such women played a decisive role in the history of women's emancipation. They could do so again today. For one thing, they are numerous. There are millions of pro-life evangelical and Catholic women in the United States. Many of them are already galvanized, and more could be, around the righteous and humane causes of women in the developing world. Once they mobilize and ally themselves with progressive forces, and with women's groups across the globe, history suggests they will prevail.

My advice to today's young women: Take back feminism. Restore its lost history. Make the movement attractive once again to the majority of American women who cherish their rights but do not wish to be liberated from their femininity—or from their fathers and brothers, husbands and sons, their male colleagues and neighbors and friends. And then make common cause with women who have not yet felt so much as a ripple of freedom, let alone two major waves. Throughout the developing world, an irresistible force of self-directed, valiant women is colliding in an epic struggle with the so-far-immovable object of patriarchal tyranny. That clash, if it turns out well, will have repercussions at least as great as those of historic Western feminism. Helping these women to succeed would give today's Western feminism something it has lacked for many years: a contemporary purpose worthy of its illustrious past.

One final suggestion. Should a pollster ask, "Are you a feminist?" say, "Yes, I am a freedom feminist!"

ENDNOTES

[1] See "Poll: Women's Movement Worthwhile," CBS News, February 11, 2009, available at http://www.cbsnews. com/2100-500160_162-965224.html; "Feminism—What's in a Name?" The Gallup Organization, September 3, 2002, available at http://www.gallup.com/poll/6715/feminism-whats-name.aspx; and "The Barrier That Didn't Fall," Daily Beast, November 18, 2008, available at http://www.tdbimg. com/upload/pdfs/TheBarrierThatDidntFall.pdf (all accessed August 19, 2012).

[2] Amanda Hess, "Enough with the Feminist Police," *Slate*, December 4, 2012, available at http://www.slate.com/ blogs/xx_factor/2012/12/04/katy_perry_says_she_s_not_a_feminist_when_are_we_going_to_stop_asking_that.html; Hillary Reinsberg, "Six Famous Women Who Say They're Not Feminists," Buzzfeed, August 20, 2012, available at http:// www.buzzfeed.com/hillaryreinsberg/6-famous-women-who-say-theyre-not-feminists; Deborah Solomon, "Case Closed: Questions for Sandra Day O'Connor," *New York Times*, March 16, 2009, available at http://www.nytimes.com/2009/03/22/ magazine/22wwln-q4-t.html (all accessed February 28, 2013).

[3] Sharon Jayson, "As NOW Marks 45 Years, Is Feminism over the Hill?" *USA Today*, October 26, 2011, available at http://yourlife.usatoday.com/mind-soul/story/2011-10-26/ As-NOW-marks-45-years-is-feminism-over-the-hill/ 50939774/1 (accessed January 19, 2012).

[4] Eve Ensler, "Vagina Warriors: An Emerging Paradigm, An Emerging Species" (Radcliffe Institute, Cambridge, Massachusetts, December 2003), lecture available through the Radcliffe Institute.

[5] Jessica Valenti, "For Women in America, Equality Is Still an Illusion," *Washington Post*, February 21, 2010, available at http://www.washingtonpost.com/wp-dyn/content/article/2010/02/19/AR2010021902049.html (accessed April 17, 2012).

[6] Bell hooks, *Feminist Theory from Margin to Center*, 2nd ed. (Brooklyn, NY: Sound End Press, 2000), p. 114.

[7] Ibid., p. 94.

[8] Ibid., p. 8.

[9] See, for example, testimonials available through The Virtue Foundation's "Advancing Women Transforming Lives Project," available at http://www.virtuefoundation.org/cms/front_content.php?idcat=71; see also Vital Voices, available at http://www.vitalvoices.org/; and the Women in the World Foundation, available at http://womenintheworld.org/.

[10] The term "feminism" was not used in the eighteenth and early nineteenth centuries. I am using it anachronistically. For purposes of this text, I will follow the broad dictionary definition of feminism as "organized activity on behalf of women's rights and interests."

[11] Abigail Adams, *The Book of Abigail and John: Selected Letter of the Adams Family, 1762–1784* (Cambridge, MA: Harvard University Press, 1975).

[12] Mary Wollstonecraft, *A Vindication of the Rights of Woman* (New York: W.W. Norton & Company, 1975), p. 37.

[13] Simon Schama, *A History of Britain*, DVD, 2002.

[14] Ibid., p. 221.

[15] Ayaan Hirsi Ali, *Infidel* (New York: Free Press, 2007), p. 295.

[16] Mitzi Myers, "Reform or Ruin: 'A Revolution in Female Manners,'" *Studies in Eighteenth-Century Culture*, vol. II (Madison, WI: University of Wisconsin Press, 1982), p. 209.

[17] Anne Stott, *Hannah More: The First Victorian* (Oxford, UK: Oxford University Press, 2003), p. 146.

[18] Ibid, p. vii.

[19] Lynne Agress, *The Feminine Irony: Women in Early-Nineteenth-Century English Literature* (New York: University Press of America, 1978), p. 48.

[20] Stott, *Hannah More: The First Victorian*, p. 6.

[21] Ibid., p. 281.

22 Ibid., p. 35.

23 Ibid., p. 224.

24 Ibid., p. 224.

25 Anne K. Mellor, "Mary Wollstonecraft's *A Vindication of the Rights of Woman* and the Women Writers of Her Day," in *The Cambridge Companion to Mary Wollstonecraft* (Cambridge, UK: Cambridge University Press, 2002), p. 148.

26 Anne K. Mellor, *Mothers of the Nation: Women's Political Writing in England, 1780–1830* (Bloomington: University of Indiana Press, 2000), p. 29.

27 Mellor, "Mary Wollstonecraft's *A Vindication of the Rights of Woman*," p. 149.

28 Ibid. See also F. K. Prochaska, *Women and Philanthropy in Nineteenth-Century England* (Oxford: Clarendon Press, 1980), p. 227.

29 Mellor, *Mothers of the Nation*, p. 15.

30 Ibid.

31 William Richardson, "Sentimental Journey of Hannah More: Propagandist and Shaper of Victorian Attitudes," *Revolutionary World*, Vols. 11–13 (Amsterdam: Grumuner, 1975), pp. 228–39.

[32] Elizabeth Kowaleski-Wallace, *Their Father's Daughters: Hannah More, Maria Edgeworth and Patriarchal Complicity* (Oxford: Oxford University Press, 1991), pp. 5, 12. See also Mellor, *Mothers of the Nation*, p. 17.

[33] Ken Burns and Paul Barnes, *Not for Ourselves Alone: The Story of Elizabeth Cady Stanton and Susan B. Anthony* (PBS, 1999).

[34] Ruth Bordin, *Frances Willard: A Biography* (Chapel Hill: University of North Carolina Press, 1986), p. 5.

[35] Carl Degler, *At Odds: Women and the Family in America from the Revolution to the Present* (Oxford: Oxford University Press, 1980), p. 316.

[36] Mellor, "Mary Wollstonecraft's *A Vindication of the Rights of Woman*," p. 14.

[37] Ellen C. DuBois, ed., *The Elizabeth Cady Stanton–Susan B. Anthony Reader* (Boston: Northeastern Press, 1981), p. 247.

[38] Suzanne M. Marilley, *Woman Suffrage and the Origins of Liberal Feminism in the United States, 1820–1920* (Cambridge, MA: Harvard University Press, 1996), p. 98.

[39] Degler, *At Odds: Women and the Family in America from the Revolution to the Present*, p. 347.

[40] Ibid., p. 346.

[41] Ibid., p. 346.

[42] Ibid., p. 350.

[43] Alexis de Tocqueville, *Democracy in America*, vol. 2 (New York: D. Appelton and Company, 1904), p. 701.

[44] Bordin, *Frances Willard: A Biography*, p. 10.

[45] Ruth Bordin, *Woman and Temperance: The Quest for Power and Liberty, 1893–1900* (Philadelphia: Temple University Press, 1981), p. 157.

[46] Ross Evans Paulson, *Liberty, Equality and Justice: Civil Rights, Women's Rights and the Regulation of Business, 1865–1932* (Durham, NC: Duke University Press, 1997), p. 95.

[47] Bordin, *Woman and Temperance*, pp. 3–4.

[48] Marilley, *Woman Suffrage and the Origins of Liberal Feminism in the United States, 1820–1920*, p. 154. See also Janet Zollinger Giele, *Two Paths to Women's Equality* (New York: Simon & Schuster, 1995), p. 105.

[49] Quoted by Willard Sorority, Nebraska Wesleyan University, available at http://willardsorority.org/frances5.html.

[50] Bordin, *Woman and Temperance*, p. 159.

[51] Elizabeth Warnock Fernea, *In Search of Islamic Feminism: One Woman's Global Journey* (New York: Random House, 1998), p. 415.

[52] See for example, Isobel Coleman, *Paradise beneath Her Feet: How Women Are Transforming the Middle East* (New York: Council on Foreign Relations, 2010).

[53] Albert Shaw, *Review of Reviews*, Vol. 6, August 1892–January 1893.

[54] Giele, *Two Paths to Women's Equality*, p. 198.

[55] Jane J. Mansbridge, *Why We Lost the ERA* (Chicago: University of Chicago Press, 1986), p. 44.

[56] Sheila Tobias, *Faces of Feminism* (New York: Harper Collins, 1997), p. 99.

[57] Sara M. Evans, *Tidal Wave: How Women Changed America at Century's End* (New York: Free Press), p. 63.

[58] *United States v. Mitchell*, 403 U.S. 190 (1971).

[59] *Phillips v. Martin Marietta Corp.*, 400 U.S. 542 (1971).

[60] *Frontiero v. Richardson*, 411 U.S. 677 (1973).

[61] *Cleveland Board of Education v. LaFleur*, 414 U.S. 632 (1974).

[62] *Taylor v. Louisiana*, 419 U.S. 522 (1975).

[63] Text of ERA, available at http://www. equalrightsamendment.org/overview.htm (accessed March 9, 2012).

[64] Flora Davis, *Moving the Mountain: The Women's Movement in America since 1960* (Urbana: University of Illinois Press, 1999), p. 131.

[65] *New York Times*, August 12, 1970, p. 40. Quoted in Davis, *Moving the Mountain: The Women's Movement in America since 1960*, p. 127.

[66] Ibid.

[67] Gail Collins, *When Everything Changed: The Amazing Journey of American Women from 1960 to the Present* (Boston: Back Bay Books, 2010), p. 221.

[68] Personal note to me from Ms. Schlafly, February 24, 2012.

[69] Joan Hoff-Wilson, ed., *Rights of Passage: The Past and Future of the ERA* (Bloomington: Indiana University Press, 1986), p. 83.

[70] Collins, *When Everything Changed: The Amazing Journey of American Women from 1960 to the Present*, p. 220.

[71] Betty Friedan, *The Feminine Mystique* (1963; New York: W. W. Norton, 2001), pp. 423–25.

[72] Eva Moscowitz, "'It's Good to Blow Your Top': Women's Magazine and a Discourse of Discontent, 1945–1954," *Journal of Women's History* 8, no. 3 (1996): pp. 66–77.

[73] See for example, bell hooks, *Feminist Theory from Margin to Center* (Cambridge, MA: South End Press, 1984 and 2000), p. 2.

[74] Alvin Toffler, quote on cover of *The Feminine Mystique*.

[75] Donald T. Critchlow, *Phyllis Schlafly and Grassroots Conservatism: A Woman's Crusade* (Princeton, NJ: Princeton University Press, 2005), p. 218.

[76] Ibid., pp. 226–27.

[77] William F. Buckley Jr., "The Equal Rights Amendment," *The Firing Line* (Southern Educational Communications Association, 1973), original air date April 15, 1973. Transcript from the Hoover Institution Library, Stanford University.

[78] Ibid.

[79] Hoff-Wilson, ed., *Rights of Passage: The Past and Future of the ERA*, p. 47.

[80] *Firing Line*, transcript, p. 1.

[81] Ibid., p. 3.

[82] "Do Americans Give Women a Fighting Chance?" Gallup Organization, June 14, 2005, available at http://www.gallup.com/poll/16810/americans-give-women-fighting-chance.aspx (accessed January 27, 2012). This poll shows Americans divided on whether or not women should be *allowed* into combat. NOW and other ERA supporters were promoting something more extreme: women drafted into combat on a par with men.

[83] *Revolution: Tomorrow Is NOW* (New York: NOW, 1973), p. 5. (This National Organization for Women policy pamphlet was compiled by Mary Samis, Tish Sommers, Marjorie Suelzle, and Nan Wood.)

[84] Joseph Lelyveld, *New York Times Magazine* (April 17, 1977), quoted on Phyllis Schlafly's website, available at http://www.eagleforum.org/misc/bio.html (accessed March 6, 2012).

[85] Critchlow, *Phyllis Schlafly and Grassroots Conservatism: A Woman's Crusade*, p. 237.

[86] Hoff-Wilson, ed., *Rights of Passage: The Past and Future of the ERA*, p. 47.

[87] Sharon Whitney, *The Equal Rights Amendment* (New York: Franklin Watts, 1984), p. 66.

[88] Ibid., p. 89.

[89] Hoff-Wilson, ed., *Rights of Passage: The Past and Future of the ERA*, p. 74.

[90] Jane J. Mansbridge, *Why We Lost the ERA* (Chicago: University of Chicago Press, 1986), p. 3.

[91] Cited in "Points to Ponder," *Reader's Digest* (March 26, 1996), p. 32.

[92] "The Harried Life of the Working Mother," Pew Research Center, October 1, 2009, available at http://www.pewsocialtrends.org/2009/10/01/the-harried-life-of-the-working-mother/ (accessed March 9, 2012).

[93] William James, *The Varieties of Religious Experience: A Study in Human Nature* (Rockville, MD: Arc Manor, 2008), p. 267.

[94] See, for example, David Geary, *Male, Female: The Evolution of Human Sex Differences* (Washington, DC: American Psychological Association, 2010); Simon Baron-Cohen, *The Essential Difference: The Truth about the Male and Female Brain* (New York: Basic Books, 2003); Jerre Levy and Doreen Kimura, "Men, Women and the Sciences," in Christina Hoff Sommers, ed., *The Science on Women and Science* (Washington, DC: AEI Press, 2010); Marco Del Giudice, Tom Booth, and Paul Irwing, *PLoS ONE*, "The Distance between Mars and Venus: Measuring Global Sex Differences in Personality," available at http://www.plosone.org/article/info:doi/10.1371/journal.pone.0029265 (accessed August 20, 2012).

[95] David P. Schmitt et al., "Why Can't a Man Be More Like a Woman? Sex Differences in Big Five Personality Traits across 55 Cultures," *Journal of Personality and Social Psychology* 94 (2008): pp. 168–82.

[96] John Tierney, "As Barriers Disappear, Some Gender Gaps Widen," *New York Times*, September 8, 2008, http://www.nytimes.com/2008/09/09/science/09tier.html?_r=0 (accessed April 5, 2013).

[97] Evans, *Tidal Wave: How Women Changed America at Century's End*, p. 174.

[98] Virginia Held, "Feminism and Epistemology: Recent Work on the Connection between Gender and Knowledge," *Philosophy and Public Affairs* (Summer 1985): p. 296.

[99] Ibid., p. 297.

[100] Catharine MacKinnon, "Desire and Power: A Feminist Perspective," in Cary Nelson and Lawrence Grossberg, eds., *Marxism and the Interpretation of Culture* (Chicago: University of Illinois Press, 1988), p. 110.

[101] See Daphne Patai and Noretta Koertge, *Professing Feminism: Education and Indoctrination in Women's Studies* (New York: Lexington Books, 2003).

[102] Margaret Andersen, *Thinking about Women* 9th ed. (Upper Saddle River, NJ: Pearson, 2011), pp. 374–93.

[103] Hooks, *Feminist Theory from Margin to Center*, p. 114.

[104] Ibid., p. 9.

[105] Ibid., p. 89.

[106] See, for example, Bordin, *Frances Willard: A Biography*, pp. 216–17.

[107] Quote from Women in the World Summit, New York City, March 10, 2012. See Melinda Liu, "Burmese Spring or Phony Thaw?" Daily Beast, March 10, 2012, http://www.thedailybeast.com/articles/2012/03/10/burmese-spring-or-phony-thaw.html (accessed August 14, 2012).

[108] See, for example, Allison Jaggar, Feminist Politics and Human Nature (Totowa, NJ: Rowman and Littlefield, 1988); Andersen, *Thinking about Women*, pp. 374–94; hooks, *Feminist Theory from Margin to Center*.

[109] Patai and Koertge, *Professing Feminism: Education and Indoctrination in Women's Studies*, p. xiv.

[110] Ibid., p. 38.

[111] Christine Stolba [now Rosen], "Lying in a Room of One's Own: How Women's Studies Textbooks Miseducate Students" (Washington, DC : Independent Women's Forum, 2002), p. 6, available at http://www.iwf.org/files/d8dcafa439b9c20386c05f94834460ac.pdf (accessed March 6, 2012).

[112] Joni Seager, *The Penguin Atlas of Women in the World*, 4th ed. (New York: Penguin Books, 2009).

[113] Ibid. American Library Association, Gloria Steinem, and *Washington Post* comments are quoted on the book jacket.

[114] Ibid.

[115] Ibid., pp. 18–19.

[116] Ibid.

[117] Ibid., pp. 28–29.

[118] See, for example, Joan Zorza, "Women Battering: High Costs and the State of the Law," in *Domestic Violence Law*, 3rd ed., ed. Nancy Lemon (St. Paul, MN: West: Thomson Reuters, 2009), p. 11. See also Hunter College Women's Studies Collective, *Women's Realities, Women's Choices: An Introduction to Women's Studies*, 3rd ed. (New York: Oxford University Press, 2005), p. 358.

[119] "National Estimates of Nonfatal Injuries Treated in Hospital Emergency Departments—United States, 2000," Centers for Disease Control (May 4, 2001), available at http://www.cdc.gov/mmwr/preview/mmwrhtml/mm5017a4.htm (accessed March 6, 2012). See also Michael Rand, "Violence-Related Injuries Treated in Hospital Emergency Departments," United States Department of Justice, Bureau of Justice Statistics Special Report (August 1997), available at http://www.ojp.usdoj.gov/bjs/pub/pdf/vrithed.pdf (accessed March 6, 2012). In a reply to my personal inquiry to the Centers for Disease Control, statistician Janey Hsiao replied, "Among ED [Emergency Department] visits made by females, the percent of having physical abuse by spouse or partner is 0.02 percent in 2003 and 0.01 percent in 2005." Date: April 2, 2009.

[120] Christina Hoff Sommers, "Persistent Myths in Feminist Scholarship," *Chronicle of Higher Education*, June 29, 2009, available at http://www.aei.org/article/society-and-culture/race-and-gender/persistent-myths-in-feminist-scholarship/ (accessed March 9, 2012). "Myths or Facts in Feminist Scholarship? An Exchange between Nancy K.D. Lemon and Christina Hoff Sommers," *Chronicle of Higher Education*, August 10, 2009, available at http://chronicle.com/article/Domestic-Violence-a/47940/ (accessed March 9, 2012).

[121] "An Analysis of Reasons for the Disparity in Wages between Men and Women," CONSAD Research Group, available at http://www.consad.com/content/reports/Gender%20 Wage%20Gap%20Final%20Report.pdf (accessed March 9, 2012).

[122] Midwest Pharmacy Workforce Research Consortium, "2009 National Pharmacies Workplace Survey" (Alexandria, VA: Pharmacy Manpower Project, 2010).

[123] Eduardo Porter, "Motherhood Still a Cause of Pay Inequality," *New York Times*, June 12, 2012, http://www. nytimes.com/2012/06/13/business/economy/motherhood-still-a-cause-of-pay-inequality.html?_r=1 (accessed June 20, 2012).

[124] AAUW, *Behind the Pay Gap*, 2007, p. 18. Buried in the report is this statement: "After accounting for all factors known to affect wages, about one-quarter of the gap remains unexplained and may be attributed to discrimination" (emphasis added). As Steve Chapman noted in *Reason*, "Another way to put it is that three-quarters of the gap clearly has innocent causes—and that we actually don't know whether discrimination accounts for the rest." Available at http:// reason.com/archives/2010/08/19/the-truth-about-the-pay-gap (accessed June 20, 2012).

[125] Ibid., p. 3.

[126] National Organization for Women, "Women Deserve Equal Pay," http://www.now.org/issues/economic/factsheet.html (accessed June 20, 2012).

[127] Available at http://www.ncrw.org/about-council (accessed April 5, 2012).

[128] *The Economist*, "Women and Work," available at http://www.economist.com/debate/overview/219 (accessed April 5, 2012).

[129] Available at http://www.ncrw.org/member-organizations/presidents-circle (accessed April 5, 2012).

[130] "Gains and Gaps: A Look at the World's Women" (New York: National Council for Research on Women, 2006), p. 4.

[131] Available at http://www.ncrw.org/programs/3901/30th-anniversary (accessed April 5, 2012).

[132] From AAUW president Linda Hallman, available at http://www.aauwnj.org/Newsletters/Fall08Garden_Statement.pdf (accessed April 6, 2012).

[133] Text of H.R. 1338 (110th), available at http://www.govtrack.us/congress/bills/110/hr1338/text (accessed March 27, 2012).

[134] "Paycheck Fairness Act Fact Sheet," National Association of Manufacturers et al., available at http://www.nam.org/~/media/16AD67E22CE24D78A870C79C42EEC825/Letter__Senate_Paycheck_Fairness_0910.pdf (accessed March 27, 2012). Letter Opposing H.R. 12, the "Paycheck Fairness Act," U.S. Chamber of Commerce, available at http://www.uschamber.com/issues/letters/2009/letter-opposing-hr-12-paycheck-fairness-act (accessed March 27, 2012).

[135] "Paycheck Fairness Act: A Flawed Approach to Job Bias," Washington Post, September 28, 2010, available at http://www.washingtonpost.com/wp-dyn/content/article/2010/09/27/AR2010092705409.html (accessed March 6, 2012). "Bill Takes on Disturbing Pay Gap—But Offers Flawed Remedies," *Boston Globe*, November 19, 2010, available at http://www.boston.com/bostonglobe/editorial_opinion/editorials/articles/2010/11/17/bill_takes_on_disturbing_pay_gap_but_offers_flawed_remedies/ (accessed August 16, 2012).

[136] Sunlen Miller, "Senate Fails to Advance the Paycheck Fairness Act," ABC News, June 5, 2012, available at http://abcnews.go.com/blogs/politics/2012/06/senate-fails-to-advance-the-paycheck-fairness-act/ (accessed April 12, 2012).

137 The Women in the World Summit, 2012. For all references to the summit, see http://www.thedailybeast.com/articles/2012/03/08/women-in-the-world-video-highlights.html (accessed April 12, 2012).

138 Lydia Saad, "Americans Still Split along 'Pro-Choice,' 'Pro-Life' Lines," Gallup, May 23, 2011, http://www.gallup.com/poll/147734/Americans-Split-Along-Pro-Choice-Pro-Life-Lines.aspx (accessed April 12, 2012).

139 Diana Furchtgott-Roth, *Women's Figures*, 2nd ed. (Washington, DC: AEI Press, 2012).

140 Stephen J. Ceci and Wendy M. Williams, *The Mathematics of Sex: How Biology and Society Conspire to Limit Talented Women and Girls* (New York: Oxford University Press, 2010).

141 See Natalia A. Kolesnikova and Yang Liu, "The Gender Wage Gap May Be Much Smaller Than Most Think," *The Regional Economist*, October 2011; An Analysis of Reasons for the Disparity in Wages between Men and Women," CONSAD Research Group, January 12, 2009, http://www.consad.com/content/reports/Gender%20Wage%20Gap%20Final%20Report.pdf (accessed March 9, 2012); Kenneth R. Ahern and Amy K. Dittmar, "The Changing of the Boards: The Impact on Firm Valuation of Mandated Female Board Representation," May 20, 2011, Social Science Review Network, available at http://papers.ssrn.com/sol3/papers.cfm?abstract_id=1364470 (accessed September 24, 2012); Joshua L. Rosenbloom et al., "Why Are There So Few Women

in Information Technology? Assessing the Role of Personality in Career Choices," *Journal of Economic Psychology* 29, no. 4 (2008): pp. 543–54.

[142] Jennifer L. Lawless and Richard L. Fox, "Men Rule: The Continued Under-Representation of Women in US Politics, January 2012," Women and Politics Institute, available at http://www.american.edu/spa/wpi/upload/2012-Men-Rule-Report-web.pdf (accessed October 7, 2012).

[143] Quotations from Ellen de Bruin from Caroline Brothers, "Why Dutch Women Don't Get Depressed," *New York Times*, June 6, 2007, available at http://www.nytimes.com/2007/06/06/arts/06iht-happy.1.6024209.html (accessed July 24, 2012); and Claire Ward, "How Dutch Women Got to Be the Happiest in the World," *Maclean's*, August 19, 2011, available at http://www2.macleans.ca/2011/08/19/the-feminismhappiness-axis (accessed October 7, 2012).

[144] "Concluding Observations of the Committee on the Elimination of Discrimination against Women: The Netherlands," available at http://www2.ohchr.org/english/bodies/cedaw/docs/co/CEDAW-C-NLD-CO-5.pdf (accessed March 27, 2012).

[145] Jessica Olien, "Going Dutch," *Slate*, November 15, 2010, available at http://www.slate.com/articles/double_x/doublex/2010/11/going_dutch.html (accessed March 9, 2010).

[146] Ibid.

[147] Caitlin Moran, *How to Be a Woman* (New York: Harper, 2012), p. 83.

[148] Ibid., pp. 82–3.

ACKNOWLEDGMENTS

Many thanks to my American Enterprise Institute research assistants and interns who contributed mightily to this project: Caroline Kitchens, Keriann Hopkins, Emily Jashinsky, Geneva Ruppert, and Harrison Dietzman. Special thanks are also owed to the incomparable Claudia Anderson for reading and editing the entire manuscript.

I also owe a special debt of gratitude to several scholars whose ideas were indispensable to this book. These include Janet Zollinger Giele (Brandeis), Ruth Bordin (University of Michigan), Anne Mellor (UCLA), Anne Stott (Open University), the late Mitzi Myers (UCLA), Daphne Patai (University of Massachusetts), and Christine Rosen (Ethics and Public Policy Center). They may not agree with all of my interpretations or accept all the precepts of freedom feminism, but I am indebted to them for their brilliant and meticulous scholarship.

I could not have written this book without the unstinting support of the American Enterprise Institute. I am especially grateful to Henry Olsen, Greg Lane, Karin Agness, Josh Good, Sterling Emerling, and Christy Sadler.

Finally, thanks are owed to my dear friend Roger Scruton. The ideas of this book were developed from an article he invited me to write for the *American*

Spectator in 2008 entitled "Feminism and Freedom." Without Roger's encouragement I may never have discovered the lost heroines, Hannah More and Frances Willard.

Christina Hoff Sommers is a resident scholar at the American Enterprise Institute. She was a professor of philosophy at Clark University from 1981 to 1996. Sommers specializes in ethics and contemporary moral theory and has published many scholarly articles in such journals as the *Journal of Philosophy* and the *New England Journal of Medicine*. Her textbook, *Vice and Virtue in Everyday Life*, currently in its ninth edition, is a bestseller in college ethics. She became known to the wider public as the author of *Who Stole Feminism? How Women Have Betrayed Women* (Touchstone Books, 1995). Her book *The War against Boys* (Touchstone Books, 2001) received widespread attention and praise and was excerpted for a cover story in the *Atlantic Monthly*. It was included in the *New York Times'* "Notable Books of the Year." She also coauthored *One Nation under Therapy* (St. Martin's Press, 2005) with Sally Satel, M.D., and is the editor of *The Science on Women and Science* (AEI Press, 2009). Sommers' articles have appeared in the *Wall Street Journal*, the *New York Times*, the *Washington Post*, the *Boston Globe*, *USA Today*, *Weekly Standard*, *National Review*, the *Economist*, the *New Republic*, and the *American*. The second edition of *The War against Boys: How Misguided Policies Are Harming Our Young Men* will be published in August 2013 (Simon and Schuster).